Who's
AT THE
DOOR?

Who's
AT THE
DOOR?

A MEMOIR OF ME
AND THE MISSIONARIES

DAN HARRINGTON

CFI
SPRINGVILLE, UT

ISBN 13: 978-1-59955-421-1

Published by CFI, an imprint of Cedar Fort, Inc.,
2373 W. 700 S., Springville, UT 84663
Distributed by Cedar Fort, Inc., www.cedarfort.com

LIBRARY OF CONGRESS CATALOGING-IN-PUBLICATION DATA

Harrington, Dan, 1978-
  Who's at the door? : a memoir of me and the missionaries / Dan Harrington.
  p. cm.
  ISBN 978-1-59955-421-1
  1. Mormon missionaries. I. Title.

  BX8661.H27 2010
  248.2'4092--dc22
  [B]

                     2010012532

Cover design by Amy Hackett
Cover design © 2010 by Lyle Mortimer
Edited and typeset by Melissa J. Caldwell

Printed in the United States of America

10 9 8 7 6 5 4 3 2 1
Printed on acid-free paper

This work is dedicated to

THE ELDERS
who became my friends,

THE INVESTIGATORS
*who treat their missionaries
with kindness,*

AND MY MOTHER,
*the first person to teach me
about the love of Jesus Christ.*

CONTENTS

NOTE FROM THE AUTHOR

It is not my intention to advocate for or against a particular church, but merely to share my experience the way I remember it. Some events may have been shortened or re-ordered for better narrative flow. Being a church investigator can often be a solitary experience, and I hope this story helps other investigators feel a little less alone.

1.

A REASON FOR YOU, A MOTIVE FOR ME

"CAN YOU TELL ME WHAT a prophet is?"

The question came from one of the two young men sitting on my clay-colored sofa. Dressed in white shirts, black slacks, and conservative ties, they were easy to identify even without the name tags—Mormons. It looked like they had stepped right off the set of *Leave It to Beaver*.

I lived on the second floor of a yellow duplex in a quiet neighborhood, where the homes were spaced a little too close together for my taste. This was Augusta, the capital of Maine, a state where humans were an endangered species. The forest outnumbered the people sixteen to one.

By local standards, though, Augusta was a fair-sized city. It boasted more than twenty thousand residents, and the population swelled when commuters came from a patchwork of rural towns to work each morning.

It was January 2007—the worst month of winter when the snow is piled high along the roads and Christmas is a memory. The weather was brutal that year, offering the kind of cold that turns your nose red as soon as you step outside. It was in that cold that I met the missionaries, and now they were in my house, on my sofa, and talking to me.

They wanted to convert me. That part was obvious. But I had a few questions to ask. I just needed to wait for my chance. In the meantime, I guess, they had questions for me.

"I never thought about it. Someone who makes a prophecy," I said.

"That's one thing a prophet can do, but a prophet's main goal is to testify of Christ. He has God's authority to lead people," the young man said.

His name tag read Elder Luke. "Elder" wasn't really his name but rather a title used to address full-time missionaries. Elder Luke carried himself with a kind of maturity that I had forgotten a twenty-year-old could possess. He spoke deliberately, as if each word was thought out in advance. For that reason, he reminded me of Spock from *Star Trek*.

And his question surprised me.

I had never thought too much about prophets. As far as I was concerned, they were associated with Old Testament times, precursors to Christ, nothing more. I had studied religious history in college and always found the subject fascinating, but I had never read much about the Mormons, or Latter-Day Saints (LDS), as is the proper term.

That was until last night. Since the missionaries were coming over, I dove into research mode. One doctrine really cried out for attention. It was so radically different from any other denomination that it sent shock waves through the Christian community.

Forget this prophet stuff. I had a better issue to discuss. Well, technically two. One was personal, but this one was academic. I'd get to the big question later.

"Excuse me," I said. "I don't mean to be rude, but there's something I really want to know."

"What is it?" the other elder asked. At over six feet tall, he was the biggest guy in the room. His blond hair and golden boy looks screamed, "I'm an all-American." And although he looked like he would have been a popular jock in high school, he lacked the arrogance I might have expected. In its place was an amicable smile that offset his companion's stoic speech. His name was Elder Childs.

"Exaltation," I said. "Is it true you think people can become gods?"

"We think it's possible to become like God," he said.

"Can you point to some scripture verses—biblical verses—to support that idea?"

"I honestly wasn't prepared for that question, Dan. I'll need to look it up, but one thing people don't understand is that we'll always be subject to God. He'll always be our Father."

When Elder Childs said he wasn't prepared, I realized that I had been leaning forward in my seat. I sat back and let his words sink in. I never expected him to say he'd have to look the answer up, but I liked it. It meant he was honest to the point of humility. That's a rare trait, especially in a young man.

"Next time we can bring some specific scriptures about it," Elder Childs said.

"Next time? You mean you come back?"

"Yes," he said. "If you let us."

And Elder Childs wanted to return. I could see it in his eyes. From his tone, I could tell it wasn't a challenge. He didn't want to debate or get the upper hand, the way a lot of Christians do when they read the Bible. Instead, he looked concerned.

"I guess that's all right. How many times do you come back?"

3

"As often as needed," Elder Luke said.

I doubted he could come that much.

During that first visit, part of me wanted to be a missionary to the elders themselves. Not of religion, but of the world. After all, they had probably come from some kind of secret compound in Utah with none of the modern conveniences most people take for granted.

"Do you know what this is?" I wanted to ask. "It's called a television. And over here—this is a microwave."

Their jaws would drop the first time I made popcorn. They'd probably think I was some great teacher like Socrates or Aristotle. But that would have to wait. First, we'd discuss this religion stuff.

Luke proceeded to talk about prophets and how they were people with special roles in the world and had unique connections with God. He listed men like Noah, Elijah, and Moses—men all Christians recognize as important. A lot of what he said I had heard before but never paid much attention to. After all, Jesus was the center of my faith. Prophets were a footnote as far as I was concerned.

I never thought about the possibility of prophets being alive today until he told me about Joseph Smith Jr., who sounded a lot like a Catholic saint, at first. A religious man who lived in the nineteenth century, Smith claimed to have had a vision in which God spoke to him. Latter-day Saints believe he discovered a hidden record, an additional gospel known as the Book of Mormon.

I knew all that from research, but reading about it on the Web was a lame substitute to hearing about it in person, straight from the believers themselves. There was a power in the elders' words, a conviction that I didn't understand. It was so strong in Elder Luke's voice that, at times, it scared me. To him, the account was obvious, like telling a child that the sun was hot or the ocean deep. Only I wasn't a child, and I wasn't there to believe.

"So you believe Joseph Smith found these gold plates that recorded events in ancient America?" I said, repeating much of his talk.

"Yes," Luke answered.

"What language were they written in?"

"A type of reformed Egyptian," Luke said. "But what matters is that it's *true*!"

His tone became defensive at the end, and it surprised me. Looking back, I wonder if he had expected an argument. Anti-Mormons are known to ridicule the story of how the Book of Mormon came to be. Perhaps that's what he thought I would do. But I only wanted to understand the missionaries. It was a far different goal than criticizing them. I didn't blame Luke for being on guard. I didn't know him, and he didn't know me. In time, I hoped, that would change.

"Will you read the Book of Mormon and pray for yourself to know if it's true?" he asked.

"I wanted to read it anyway. But there's one more question I have for you." They both stared at me. This was it. The moment I was waiting for. "I'm a new freelance writer for the paper, and I want to write an article about you two."

Childs raised an eyebrow and turned to his companion. Luke stared at me. He was either lost in thought or sizing me up, the way men do before a fight. If he expected ill of me, clearly he needed more persuasion. "It would be a local interest piece about why you're here and what you do. I wouldn't say anything bad or mean," I explained.

If that didn't work, my next move was to offer them

chocolate. Chocolate or ice cream. Who could resist? And while they ate, I'd dazzle them with the microwave. If anything could seal the deal, that would.

"How many articles have you published?" Childs asked.

I was hoping that wouldn't come up. I groaned inside. "Well . . . ," I said. "One. I'm brand new." Ugh! What an embarrassing answer, but it was the truth. It was all I had.

"We need to discuss it with our superiors and get back to you," Elder Luke said.

I thanked them for their time, and as they left, I crossed my fingers and hoped for the best.

That night I read from the Book of Mormon for the first time. I also prayed as the missionaries had requested. It seemed harmless enough, but this is where things got murky.

In the introduction, Smith recalls how he unearthed the gold plates that would provide the basis for the book. These plates had been hidden for centuries and stood as a record of a previously unknown people who had inhabited America in ancient times. They were Jews who fled Israel, believed in Jesus, and had been visited by the Savior after his resurrection in the New Testament. It was a lot to swallow.

To most Christians, it sounded crazy—a tall tale like the adventures of Paul Bunyan and his big blue ox. Some people can't even mention the book without a smirk or quip about how foolish (or dangerous) it is. Yet, these were the same people who insisted that Noah lived several hundred years, Moses spoke to a burning bush, and that a she-bear once mauled some children because they taunted the prophet Elijah about being bald.

The fact is that if the Book of Mormon were true, it was nothing less than a miracle, and every miracle has its doubters.

I should know. I'm one of them.

But the book struck a special chord with me that night. A miracle? I brushed the text with my fingers. The idea alone held a certain power, a mystique that beckons me to this day. Smith's words felt sincere. It didn't seem like something he made up for kicks.

Of course, I didn't tell the missionaries all that. The next time they came, I kept the tone of our conversation friendly but neutral. Childs was already at ease in my home. I could tell by the way he plopped his backpack on the floor. Luke set his pack down gingerly as I took their coats and hung them on pegs in the back hall.

"Elder Childs spent his personal study time researching your question about exaltation," Luke said. "Here are Bible verses you can reference."

I wrote the list down in my notebook. This activity would become a staple of our time together. I'd sit with the Book of Mormon and Bible in my lap and keep notes of our lessons. My memory never has been the best. It's one reason I like to write.

"Have you heard back about whether or not I can write about you?" I asked.

"We have," Luke said.

"And?"

"We were talking about it on the way over here," Elder Childs said. "We think it would be okay."

Success! I didn't need the chocolate bribe or magic microwave after all. "Great! When?" I asked.

"Let's discuss this after our lesson," Elder Luke said.

"Last time we gave you a Book of Mormon. Have you read any of it?"

"Of course."

A smile grew on Elder Childs's face. "What did you read about?"

"The angel Moroni, the sword of Laban, and the prophet Lehi. And . . ."

I can't recall the rest of that visit, but I do remember a sense of excitement in the room, especially from Elder Childs. He was ready to teach, and I was willing to learn. But more important, I was ready to write.

* * *

There was only one pitfall left, one more obstacle to endure—my editor. I hadn't known Joyce very long, but she actually spoke to me when I called. Back then I didn't realize how much of a triumph that was. Some editors make me talk to a secretary or—worse yet—their voice-mail, and that's even after they publish my work. But not Joyce. She was a native of Augusta and cared about the community. I needed her to know I cared about it too.

"Thank you so much for publishing my first column. It came out great!" I said. Notice my subtle suggestion in the word *first*.

I had wanted to be a published writer ever since I could remember. Although I had a few sparse publications in years past (one poem and an article), this was another animal entirely.

When I was in college, I always felt like my life was pushing ahead, progressing toward something better than a degree. I was studying writing and religion, and I was ready to tackle the world. But after graduation, life lost its sheen. My dreams had crashed from their lofty heights into the grit of the earth. Each day revolved around the monotony of office work. My paycheck was the sun, and I had to spend each day orbiting it like a lifeless moon.

At twenty-nine years old, I knew there had to be more to life than paying bills, not to mention the faxing, filing, and a boss who could micromanage her way into the hall of fame. Waking up in the morning had become a chore, a duty rather than a desire. It's not how I wanted to live.

Years of mundane existence had crawled under my skin and set my fingers on fire with a renewed passion for the written word. I needed to see my words in print. I needed meaning in my life again.

On my knees, I had prayed to God for direction. I just needed something worthwhile to write about, something that would jump-start my career. He had sent me the missionaries.

Of course, it wasn't the type of thing I wanted to explain over the phone. A more lighthearted approach was required.

"I have another idea for a story," I said as casually as I could.

"What is it?" Joyce asked.

So far, so good. "I met these two young missionaries in our area."

"Missionaries? What kind?"

"Latter-day Saints. They're the young guys who knock on people's doors. I thought I could write about who they are and why they're here."

"Eh . . . show it to me, and we'll see, all right?"

It wasn't the most enthusiastic response, but I could work with it. As far as I was concerned, I just bought a lottery ticket, and the odds were in my favor.

It made me a little neurotic for the interview. I must

have checked my tape recorder a dozen times and spent an hour coming up with questions. Elder Childs may have been the only person more nervous than I was. When I set the tape recorder on a footstool in front of him, he stared at it like it might become a venomous snake.

"Can I take your coat?" I asked.

He pulled it tighter around his neck. "I'm comfortable with it on," he said.

Elder Luke gave me his jacket as he sat next to his companion. His expression was placid, as always, and the interview went well. I learned that Luke liked to hunt and listen to country music, while Childs enjoyed dating and was on the football team in high school. They both liked basketball. Except for their time spent as missionaries, their lives were pretty much like most young men. In fact, they even lived in regular homes, not in communes like I once suspected.

The juxtaposition of these elements would appeal to my readers. The fact that these guys knew about television and movies was unexpected, to say the least. I'm not sure what I thought about Mormons except that I carried a vague concept of them as old-fashioned pioneers whose faith was as popular as stale bread.

It was certainly not considered cool for two young men—Childs, 19, from Texas and Luke, 20, from Utah—to talk to strangers about Jesus. During their two years as missionaries, the elders tried to live in a manner that focused on faith alone. That meant teaching strangers about their church and keeping a distance from their own everyday lives. Elder Childs said it was best not to have distractions—that's why missionaries aren't allowed to call their parents except twice a year on Mother's Day and Christmas.

Elder Childs and Elder Luke as they looked in 2007.

I'd later learn that people did all sorts of rotten things to the missionaries such as giving them the finger in public or throwing garbage from their cars, and these things weren't happening in some far off place. They happened in my own hometown. That was the saddest part.

But none of the elders ever emphasized their problems. They barely mentioned them unless I asked, and I like to think their honesty had less to do with my questions and more to do with me.

When Luke and Childs left that day, they were almost as excited to see the article in print as I was. Almost.

The article nearly wrote itself, pouring out of my fingers, unlike most of my prose, which required too much thought. After I submitted my work, I couldn't wait to hear from the editor.

In the meantime, I looked into the verses Elder Childs had provided. I was shocked he could supply any. I thought he'd say exaltation was a Latter-day Saint revelation available only in the Book of Mormon, but instead he was able to offer passages from the Bible just, as I had requested. First on the list was Romans 8:16–17:

> The Spirit itself beareth witness with our spirit, that we are the children of God: And if children, then heirs; heirs of God, and joint-heirs with Christ; if so be that we suffer with him, that we may be also glorified together.

I had heard about being a co-heir with Christ before but not in this context. I had heard Baptist preachers say that Christ was a forerunner who shows what will happen to us if we follow the Lord. I always took that to mean our resurrection, but the elders saw it on a whole different level. Next on my list was John 10:31–35:

> Then the Jews took up stones again to stone him. Jesus answered them, Many good works have I shewed you from my Father; for which of those works do ye stone me? The Jews answered him, saying, For a good work we stone thee not; but for blasphemy; and because that thou, being a man, makest thyself God. Jesus answered them, Is it not written in your law, I said, Ye are gods? If he called them gods, unto whom the word of God came, and the scripture cannot be broken.

The passage referred to a psalm in the Old Testament that echoed the idea that those who received the word of God were co-heirs with Christ. This was more evidence than I ever expected, for what was an heir but a person who inherited everything someone else had?

The problem was that in this case the "someone else" was God. So it wasn't just that we would get to heaven and worship the Lord as perfected beings the way most Christians believed. We had the potential to be like God in power with the ability to form planets, create oceans, and command angels. It was far too big to consider.

The possibility of becoming like God—a god—crashed into my personal faith the way a scooter might hit a guardrail on the freeway. The Bible passages may have left a dent, but in the LDS context they had to be wrong.

They had to be.

2.

SURPRISE INVITATION

A FEW DAYS LATER, JOYCE called with her verdict on the story. "It was really interesting," she said. "Everyone knows who the missionaries are, but they don't know anything about them. You did a great job."

A great job! The review was better than I hoped.

"I have more ideas for stories," I said.

"Let's hear them."

And that was the start of my writing career. From then on, Joyce always took my calls. Soon she even started to call me. When a regular reporter was on vacation, I'd take two or more stories per week, and I was proud to be the editor's right-hand man. Over the years, I'd write about local cops, boxers, cage fighters in training, and numerous churches. It all started with the missionaries. I never forgot that.

The day my story about the elders came out, I must have bought a dozen copies of the paper. I called my parents, siblings, friends, and coworkers—anyone who would listen. I was published, and I wanted the world to know.

The thrill was like being at the apex of a roller coaster in those few enticing moments before the wild descent. Elation rushed though my body as a frantic energy. It felt like I could run a marathon without stopping for breath. Rarely had I felt such a mixture of joy and pride. If I were Leonardo DiCaprio, it would have been the moment where I declared my reign as king of the world.

I dialed the missionaries to share the news.

"Hello, this is Elder Childs."

"Elder Childs, our story is out. We're in the paper!"

"That's awesome!"

"I'll see you in over an hour. I can't wait!"

Click. I hung up without giving him a chance to reply. We already had our next appointment scheduled, but the phone rang again. Whoever it was, I already had good news to share.

"Dan, it's Elder Childs."

"We're in the paper!" I repeated the message in case he missed it the first time.

"We just wanted to know where we can get copies."

"At my house! I bought copies for you both."

"Oh, thanks so much."

"I can't wait to see you, so hurry!" I said. He chuckled and said good-bye. I could hear him relaying the message to Luke before the line went dead.

I decided to take a power walk. I needed something to pass the time, and my mind was too frantic for television or the radio. The minutes were already creeping along the clock. I had to do something.

The exercise didn't help much. Twenty minutes later, I wrung my hands and paced my living room. Every few minutes, I'd walk to my large picture window and gaze down at the street. Eventually, the missionaries' silver car pulled up. It was a little disappointing to see them in a car instead of riding the bikes their kind were so famous for, but who cared when we were in the paper?

Casting all pleasantries aside, I ran down the stairs and flung open my front door. "Hey, guys, get in here!" I said as they climbed out of the car. Elder Childs was in the passenger side. His pace quickened.

"Hey, Dan." He greeted me with a clasp of the hand. I could sense the excitement in his grip. He followed me up the stairs with Elder Luke not far behind. As soon as we reached the living room, I stuck a newspaper in the hand of Childs.

" 'Two Men on a Mission.' " He read the headline with pride. He was still at the age when it was a thrill to be called a man instead of a boy.

I opened the paper and turned to the appropriate page for him. Technically, LDS missionaries aren't supposed to read the paper, but in this case, they were making an exception. Childs plopped himself on the sofa and grinned from ear to ear.

Luke, meanwhile, fiddled with the zipper of his backpack before taking his usual spot on the sofa. I stuck a newspaper in front of him as well. He took it without looking at me.

I tried not to stare as they read, but I could hardly contain myself. To give the illusion of privacy, I crossed the archway into my kitchen and poured us each a glass of water. That's when it hit me. What if they didn't like the story? Oh, but I was sure they would.

" 'Missionaries aren't allowed to read the newspaper,' " Elder Childs quoted. "But I'm reading one right now!"

I couldn't put every detail in the article, of course. One story Elder Luke had shared at the interview disgusted me. Once, when he was knocking on doors, a man had asked him to wait at the front step while he retrieved something "special." The man came back with a gun. In usual Spock fashion, Luke dismissed the event, but hearing about it made me angry. I thought about putting it in the paper to shame the person, but I didn't. The actions of a low-life local weren't going to take away from the hard work the elders were doing.

Here were two young men spending their own money as full-time volunteers. They could have been partying, watching endless hours of MTV, or just plain dating. Instead, they chose to work as missionaries for their church. Few teenagers ever make such a commitment.

When they finished reading, I asked what they thought.

"That was very well written," Luke remarked. It sounded like a comment on the weather.

Elder Childs playfully slapped his companion on the head with his paper. "When you make the papes, you're famous!" he declared.

"I have copies for both of you to send your families. I thought they would want to see the story too," I said.

"Thank you so much," Elder Childs said. "It was awesome. The story was awesome."

Elder Luke folded his copy of the paper and placed it on the floor by his feet. "So have you read any more of the Book of Mormon?" he asked.

"I have."

Just like that he snapped the conversation back to religion, but I had a hard time paying attention. My mind wandered back to the article, wondering how many people might be reading it at that very moment.

The story was online too, and I imagined people at their desktops—a father reading it before dinner, an old lady being taught how to use the Internet finding it. A whole family could be gathered around my article, reading intently with "ooohs" and "ahhhs" as if they were watching a grand display of fireworks. It probably wasn't happening, but it made me feel good to think it could be.

"Dan, did you hear me?" Elder Childs asked.

"What?"

"I asked if you would come to church with us."

"No," I said. The answer was automatic.

"No?"

"No." I shook my head for emphasis. "I thought only members could go anyway."

It was a comforting thought too. I had Protestant friends who wanted me to attend their services. Going once meant being begged to attend over and over again. It was never a one-shot deal. The expectations were endless.

"That's the temple," Childs explained. "Anyone can come to our church."

"Anyone?"

"Yes."

I could see it now. He and Luke would start bringing the issue up until I relented. "What if I'm really bad? You don't want anyone like that visiting your church, do you?" I joked.

Elder Childs smirked. Luke offered no reaction. He just stared at me.

It was doubtful I could talk them out of it, but I didn't need to. The article was out. The interview was over. This could be a good time to part ways. They'd stop visiting sooner or later. Perhaps that time should be now.

"I think you'd like our service more than you realize," Elder Childs said. "In the first hour—"

"The *first* hour?" I interrupted. "How long is it?

"Three hours."

"Three *full* hours?"

"Yes, Dan. Please let me finish. In the first hour, members of the Church get up to speak. They share their experiences with everyone about how they feel close to the Savior. I know how much you like hearing people's stories."

Indeed, it was a novel idea. Instead of a single preacher or priest giving a sermon, regular members addressed the congregation, or ward, as the Mormons call it. I had never heard of a service like it before.

"What if someone says something blasphemous?" I asked.

"Then we all listen politely, and the bishop talks to them later," Childs said.

"Well . . . maybe one visit won't hurt."

"Good. It starts at 9:00 a.m. Now we have to get going." Luke stood and looked at his watch. I had a tendency to keep the elders longer than scheduled. That day was no exception. Plus, I knew that Luke wanted to leave before I could change my mind.

We scheduled our next visit, said our farewells, and when they were gone, I prayed that I wasn't making a big mistake.

3.

THREE FULL HOURS

SUNDAY. 8:00 A.M.

As soon as my alarm went off, I snapped awake. My mind filled with excuses, each one more lame than the last. My car broke down. I had a fever. The devil broke my alarm clock. The last one might at least get Elder Childs to laugh. Not Elder Luke, though. He'd see right through it. Oh, who was I kidding? They both would.

I forced myself out of bed, undressed, and got into the shower. Normally, I banished my doubts by concentrating on something frivolous like a scene from one of my favorite movies.

That morning I recalled the kitchen sequence from *Jurassic Park,* when the children hide from hungry raptors with only a ladle as a weapon. Soon they were discovered and a pair of flesh-devouring dinosaurs was on their trail.

I wasn't being chased by raptors. I had missionaries after me. By comparison, visiting a new church would be easy.

In my black slacks, blue shirt, and tie, I zipped my winter jacket up and left my apartment with few moments to spare. About an inch of snow had fallen during the night, and I stepped carefully down my driveway to avoid any hidden patches of ice. Although the congregation was known as the Augusta Ward, the building was located in Farmingdale, a good fifteen minutes away.

As I drove, other places of worship seemed to leap out at me. Penny Memorial Baptist Church, St. Augustine's, and South Parish Congregational Church all had imaginary neon signs above them with yellow arrows that pointed for me to stop. If I were visiting any one of them, I would have arrived already, but of course, the Mormons had to be out of town. Yuck.

The LDS church was easier to find than I expected. Located on a small side street, it was nestled among a handful of homes that formed a private neighborhood off the main drag. A slim white steeple poked out from the roof. I'd later learn—much to my dismay—that it was merely a decoration. No one could go into the steeple, and I found that depressing. As a child, I had always wanted to explore the highest peaks of churches, to look out and see the world in a way I imagined God might. It was silly, of course, but realizing it was impossible to see from that height, at least without a ladder, offered a hue of regret.

The rest of the structure was made of brick and was just one story high. It reminded me of a conference center or business office rather than a house of worship. But that was due to my own prejudice.

I was used to Gothic-style Catholic churches with their tall spires and arched doorways framed in stone. This church, on the other hand, was something new to experience, and there was no harm in seeing what that was. If people could skydive, bungee jump, or swim with sharks, I could certainly visit an LDS church. As I pulled into the parking lot, I wished I hadn't thought of that last analogy.

Other people were still arriving. A mother rushed toward a glass door with her two young daughters in tow. They all wore conservative dresses. The mother was in black, while the girls wore bright shades of blue and white. They were dressed up but not in the old-fashioned manner some people might expect. Their clothes could have come from any store in any town. After locking my car, I took a deep breath and followed them toward the door.

A gentleman, who was perhaps in his late sixties, greeted me as I walked inside. "Welcome! Thank you for coming," he said as we shook hands.

I smiled and made my way into a narrow hall that looked like it could have been part of an elementary school. It led into a vestibule where people milled about in clusters. The missionaries were nowhere to be seen. I looked for anyone else I might know, but only one face was familiar.

A large picture of Jesus standing in the clouds caught my eye. Angels clothed in white gathered around the Savior in two great processions. Some of them blew into gold trumpets that were pointed toward the heavens as Jesus stood with his arms open in acceptance. It was a beautiful picture that reminded me of the Second Coming. I'd later learn that's exactly what it was.

Sifting through the bodies, I tried to be discreet as I navigated my way to the main room. It didn't work. Another man approached me with an outstretched hand. "Welcome! Welcome!" he said with a smile.

"Thank you," I said, and we clasped hands.

My name barely escaped my lips when another man approached. Then another and another. I could hardly take a step without someone else introducing himself and asking my name in return. It was like walking a red carpet, and everyone wanted a brief interview.

It made me anxious. The main problem was that I heard so many names in such a short time that I couldn't remember any of them. One guy was named Jon. I remembered that much.

Eventually I made my way into the main room, where long, slender lights dangled from a cathedral ceiling. Pews cut the room in half with chairs in the back for overflow. A small stage and a podium with nothing more behind it than a simple white wall was at the front of the room. It was a quaint setting but lacked the grandeur of my Catholic upbringing. No stained glass windows, no statues—not even a cross could be found.

I unzipped my coat and sat where I felt I belonged—in the back and alone. People were filing into the room, and that's when I noticed the missionaries. They were steeped in conversation with a man at the far corner. Childs was scanning the room, clearly looking for someone. His eyes lit up when he noticed me.

"Dan, it's so good to see you here," he said as he came over.

"I gave you my word I'd come," I told him.

"We're sitting in the pews," he said. "Come join us."

"That's all right. I should sit in the back."

He opened his mouth to say more, but a speaker at the head of the room called for everyone's attention.

"I'll come see you at the end of this session," he said.

The service began with a prayer and a song, and soon some young boys were heading my way with a silver platter. They stopped at the end of each pew and passed their plate into the crowd row by row.

Time to cough up some money. I reached for my wallet and thumbed through my cash. Taking out three one dollar bills, I folded them between my middle and index finger, ready to drop them in the plate.

Only when the young man came closer, I saw what he had. It wasn't a tray of money. It was a tray of communion bread. The Mormons call it the sacrament. It was a pleasant surprise. I sighed, feeling like a fool, and took some of it before passing the plate to my nearest neighbor.

"Do this in remembrance of me," I thought, recalling the Savior's words.

Catholics had to get in line to accept communion, and as much as it pained me to think this, it was also a time where people looked to see who was at church, who was wearing their Sunday best, who looked nervous, and who looked holy. My mother had long complained about such whisperings at church. I never heard any of them myself, but she was always keenly aware of hypocrisy.

Yet the simple act of bringing the bread to the congregation eliminated that spectacle. It was a small difference and one that I liked.

The boys brought the wine to us too. Only it wasn't wine; it was water. Instead of everyone drinking from a single chalice, the liquid was poured into individual cups.

Later, some members of the congregation gave talks, and while I can't remember exactly what they said, I do recall their emotion. It wasn't showy either. No one shouted "amen" or "hallelujah!"

This emotion was dignified. A man about six feet three with a shaved head talked about how God had blessed him with a wonderful wife and child. As he spoke, tears ran down his cheeks. He looked more like a quarterback than a man who would weep in public, but he thanked

God for all he had and concluded his talk in the name of Jesus.

The meeting closed with a benediction, and voices swept away the silence as people left the room in friendly conversation. The elders headed straight for me.

"Ready for round two?" Childs asked.

"I guess."

He and Luke led me down an adjacent hall and into a classroom that could have been left over from the 1950s. A blackboard was at the front of the room beside a large American flag. There were no desks, only plastic chairs, and we sat next to a row of windows that overlooked a tiny lawn draped in newly fallen snow.

A lady who may have been in her fifties entered the room. She was plump with short white curls and a bright smile. She reminded me of my childhood teachers and spoke in a pleasant voice that still commanded respect. To this day, I don't recall her name, only that she was an excellent teacher.

It was an important skill since the second hour was basically Sunday School for adults. Here potential converts and the recently baptized would gather to learn more about basic LDS doctrines like Jesus Christ's Atonement or the importance of charity. It reinforced much of what people learned from the missionaries but offered a chance to ask questions from someone other than a nineteen-year-old.

The third hour was called priesthood quorum, and it was my favorite part of the service. All the men came together to discuss a faith topic from a male perspective. The women had a similar meeting, called Relief Society, in another part of the building.

The men gathered back in the main hall where

someone asked if anyone had any news or announcements. A gentleman in the front row raised his hand.

"There's a very nice article in the paper about our missionaries. I put it on the bulletin board if anyone wants to read it," he said.

Elder Childs was sitting beside me in the pew. His hand flew up.

"And the man who wrote it is right here next to me!" he declared.

Everyone turned to look, and a few of the men motioned for me to stand. Good thing I had on my best tie. I thought maybe I should say a few words, perhaps give a speech about the missionaries or the Church, but nothing poignant came to mind, so I nodded and sat back down. Later I joked with my family that if the Mormons had asked for my autograph, I would have joined the Church right then and there.

After the meeting, several men came over to shake my hand and thank me for the article. Elder Childs smiled, happy that I was getting so much attention.

A thin teenage boy dressed in a white shirt and blue tie came over as well. Only he didn't speak to me. He asked Elder Childs something about basketball. I didn't hear exactly what.

All the young men came over then and huddled around Elder Childs. In response, he leaned back and rested his arms on the pew. I could tell he loved the attention but was trying to act casual about it. It reminded me of high school and how people gathered around the cool kids.

"You can tell you've been out in the field for a long time," Elder Childs was saying, "when you're wearing your missionary clothes even in your dreams."

The boys all laughed. "Missionaries have weird dreams," one of them said.

It was clear they looked up to Elder Childs. And why wouldn't they? In a few years, they would take his place as representatives of the Church. Talking to him offered a glimpse of the future.

When the boys dispersed, I turned to Childs. "I was wondering if I could take you and Elder Luke out to dinner. It would be my way of saying thank you for the article."

Elder Childs sat straight up. He pulled his weekly planner out and waved Elder Luke over to us. Luke had been talking with some members but excused himself from the conversation.

"Dan wants to take us out to eat to thank us for letting him do the article." His words tripped over each other.

There was a slight hesitation in his tone though, and I knew why. Elder Luke could veto the matter in a second. If so, that would be it. Adios, free feast. Elder Luke was his trainer and also known as the senior companion. That's missionary talk for the supervisor. Insert the music from *Jaws* here.

Luke stood there with a Spock-like stare.

"It's not against the rules," he said.

That was as much interest as we could get him to muster, but it was enough.

4.

TEACHERS TO FRIENDS

LIKE ALWAYS, THE MISSIONARIES arrived on time. It was one of my favorite things about them—they kept their word. The older I get, the more I realize how special that is. We took my car, and Elder Luke sat in front.

"So where do you guys want to go? I was thinking Chinese."

"If we eat Chinese, I'll only eat rice," Luke said.

"Can we do something else so Elder Luke will eat?" Childs chimed in from the back.

"Of course. It's completely up to you guys."

I offered more choices.

Augusta boasted an array of restaurants, especially on the north edge of town. When I was growing up, that section had teamed with wild grass and woods. Now it was a tourist destination named The Marketplace at Augusta. Chain restaurants dotted the area complete with a large strip mall, huge cinema, and Walmart Supercenter. It's what most people called progress. Have you ever noticed how progress goes hand-in-hand with bulldozers and pavement? It's a companionship most Mainers lament. The elders didn't know the history of the city, of course. They just knew they were hungry.

Elder Luke decided on Red Robin. He enjoyed their food and wanted his companion to try it.

"So what's new with you, Elder Luke?" I asked.

Whenever I made small talk, Childs would answer. Since Luke sat in the front, he'd be forced to carry on a conversation. Without knowing it, he had fallen into a neat little trap. He couldn't be all Spock all the time, could he?

He listed activities from knocking on doors to giving lessons. It had all the emotion of a shopping list.

With my head in conversation and my hands on the wheel, I stopped at the corner of the main road and decided there was plenty of time to pull in front of an oncoming black car.

As soon as I pressed on the gas, Elder Luke's voice died. My white Ford Escort was small but quick. It hesitated for the slightest second, and the car behind us grew large in my rearview mirror. Then, with a small jerk we sped away, out of its reach.

"What were you saying, Elder Luke?" I asked.

He didn't respond.

Instead, he studied the mirror on his side of the car. In the back, Elder Childs' eyes were wide, as if he had witnessed something amazing or terrible.

"Don't worry, I had time," I said.

Silence. I got the feeling they didn't agree.

"Don't worry, guys. We've got God to protect us. Well, God and Elder Luke," I joked. A polite chuckle came from the backseat, but we didn't talk again until we got to the restaurant.

I guess dinner and an accident wasn't their idea of fun.

Red Robin was fairly new to Augusta back then.

Pictures of movie stars speckled the walls. A human-sized Statue of Liberty greeted us with a hamburger in place of the torch. A monitor was built into a glass block in the floor, and both elders took note of it. The restaurant reminded me of Disney World with its bright red walls and glossy tables that shined. Hardly anyone was there that day, so it felt like we had the place all to ourselves. Our hostess seated us in a flash. Her dark hair was swept up in a ponytail, and she wore a huge grin as she handed us menus.

All three of us ordered water. It's the drink of choice for missionaries and people who don't like to pay two dollars for a soda. The hostess should have left right then, but she went on and on suggesting things we could order.

I wanted her to go away so I could read the menu in peace, but she lingered at the table. I noticed then that she wasn't looking at me at all. Her eyes were locked on Elder Childs. She was about his age, and the more she spoke, the more obvious it became that she was talking only to him.

But Childs didn't notice. He was reading the menu like it was scripture.

"You'd better be careful," I warned. "These guys are priests."

Elder Childs looked up, and his face turned red. The hostess laughed and returned to her post. I got a kick out of it myself, but I hoped she wouldn't spit in my food.

When the waitress arrived, I ordered a plate of nachos to share as well as a bacon cheeseburger for myself. Elder Luke ordered the same burger I did, but Childs had yet to make up his mind.

He asked the waitress what she would recommend, and I knew right then that this guy was a flirt. Perhaps he didn't mean to be. I'm sure he thought the question was harmless, but like the hostess, the waitress could barely peel her eyes off him.

Childs went along with whatever the waitress suggested, and she rushed away happy as a cheerleader.

"I feel like I'm sitting with a celebrity," I said.

"What?" Childs asked. His head was in the clouds, still pondering either the waitress or the menu.

"Wait until you see the burgers here," Luke interjected. "They're as big as a plate."

Finally, I thought, *some emotion from Spock, and all it took was red meat.*

"So you've been here before, Luke?" I asked.

"Yes, my parents sent me a gift card last Christmas. I didn't know they had Red Robin in Maine."

"I think this is the only one in the state. Do other investigators ever do things like this for you guys?"

"They've never taken us out to eat, if that's what you mean," Luke said.

"No, I mean do they ever feed you or anything like that?"

"Yes, usually the people who invite us into their lives are good people already."

In a roundabout way, it was a compliment.

The waitress set a plate crammed with crispy nachos covered in cheese, jalapeños, salsa, and sour cream on the table. My mouth watered.

"Dig in," I said.

Elder Childs attacked the plate, and I knew right then that we were kindred spirits.

"I love these jalapeños," Childs said. "They give it a little kick."

"Really? I don't even taste them," I said between chews.

"I don't either," Luke agreed.

"Well, I'm tasting this one."

Elder Luke pointed to a splash of salsa that had landed on the table in front of his companion. "Be careful that doesn't get on your shirt."

"You're always thinking practical," Childs told him. "I like it!"

We decimated the appetizer in a matter of moments. That's what happens when three hungry men eat from the same plate. A single chip was all that stood out among the crumbs. Elder Luke wiped his hands on a napkin to show he was finished. Childs stared at the chip like it might sprout legs and run.

"You can have that," I told him.

"Gladly," Childs said, snatching it from the plate.

When the main course arrived, we discovered the waitress had goofed up Luke's order as well as my own. It was something minor, like we didn't want tomatoes and there they were. Childs said nothing. He was too busy shoving steak fries in his mouth. His order was perfect. Imagine that.

"You should have waited until Luke and I had our food before you flirted with the waitress," I said.

Childs's eyes widened, and he began to cough. I thought he might choke for a minute, but he recovered with a smirk.

"So you sent the article home?" I asked.

"Yes, my parents were really excited," Childs said, grabbing for more fries. "I've had siblings on missions, but no one has ever written about them."

"Why's that?"

"They never met any writers, or at least not one like you."

"Are any of your siblings on a mission now?"

"My sister is."

"Oh, so she's a priestess?" I asked with feigned inno-
cence. I peppered a few off-the-wall comments in of our
conversations for amusement.

Elder Childs stared. "No, see in the Church—"

"I'm just kidding."

"Oh! Sometimes I can't tell when you're serious and
when you're not."

"I know. I like it that way," I said.

The meal was pleasant, and even more important, so
was the company. The elders didn't bring up religion. I
guess when you talk about church eight hours a day, you're
happy to get a break.

We left with our bellies full and our spirits high. Elder
Childs patted his stomach as we stepped into the parking
lot. Twilight had turned the sky a soft shade of pink, and the
world was a silhouette against it.

"Are you ready to find people tonight, Elder?" Childs
asked.

He sounded like an athlete psyching himself up
before a big game. Apparently the question was rhetorical,
because Elder Luke did not respond. Luke and I got in the
car, and out of habit, I locked the doors.

Suddenly, Elder Childs knocked on the window
behind me in rapid succession. The sound was frantic as if
I had just run over his foot. The car hadn't moved, so that
couldn't have happened. Still, something was wrong.

I released the lock, but for Elder Childs it wasn't fast
enough.

"I can't be away from Elder Luke," he said.

"What?" I asked.

"It's one of our rules," Luke stated.

"Why?"

"Mostly for safety reasons," Luke said.

"Well, if I had known that, I would have driven down the parking lot a little before I unlocked the door."

No one else laughed, but I did.

5.

ADVICE FROM HOME

IN THE WEEKS THAT FOLLOWED, I read everything I could about the Latter-day Saints. In college I read about various faiths, but the missionaries offered a chance to learn from real believers instead of textbooks.

Plus, I enjoyed their company.

My studies pleased the missionaries, in particular Elder Childs, who found my attention to detail impressive.

"You've been doing awesome reading the Book of Mormon," he said. "I'm surprised at how much you remember."

He later admitted that my questions kept his lessons exciting. He had never known a nonmember to pronounce the prophet Nephi's (Knee-Fi) name correctly on a first reading, note the lack of female names in the Book of Mormon, or point out that the Nephites weren't headed for the Atlantic Ocean on their journey.

"What do other investigators say about the book?" I asked.

"Sometimes they say they've been reading it, but when we ask what they read, they can't remember," he told me.

I guess by those standards, I was impressive. I also learned that the Church calls the people the missionaries teach "investigators." Being an investigator was as new to me as being a missionary was to Elder Childs.

He had only been out on his mission a few weeks when we met. I was eager to learn, and he was eager to teach. There was an excitement in our lessons, an energy that thrives when people love the Lord.

Striving for a better relationship with God was important to both of us, and to this day, I don't think I would have found the Mormons as interesting as I did if I hadn't met Elder Childs.

I was thankful for Elder Luke as well, but even after numerous visits, his personality remained hidden. Somehow he had tucked it behind his name tag, away from the world, away from me. With Childs it was obvious that he liked coming to see me, but not with Luke. And when I can't tell what people are thinking, I tend to assume the worst.

Since Elder Luke wasn't a robot—at least not technically—I prided myself on those sparse occasions when I managed to see a hint of who he was. This was usually accomplished through a joke or a tease.

Once I threatened to throw a snowball at him. Luke looked me dead in the eye and said, "I'd just throw one right back." From his tone, I could tell he was serious, perhaps a little too serious.

During that time, the missionaries started coming over more often. We ate together. We prayed together. We discussed the gospel together.

I had started meeting with them as a writer, a freelance journalist who wanted to know who they were and what their lives were like, but the more we met, the more their faith made sense.

It wasn't just a collection of outlandish doctrine like

some dissenters insisted. It was a way of life and a way to love God. It was the way they believed their Heavenly Father loved them in return.

Latter-day Saints felt that God saw the spiritual confusion in the world and re-established his church, the way it was always meant to be. They called this the Restoration. It wasn't a human gesture. It was a sign from the divine hand of God that he cared about his children. He had sent us Jesus Christ to redeem us. He had left us the Bible as a guide, but his infinite love didn't end there.

That's why, the Latter-day Saints might say, God appeared to Joseph Smith Jr.—not to make Smith important, but to make God's message about the Savior and the Church clear.

So what were the arguments against the missionaries: that God didn't send holy people to lead his church, that God no longer revealed his will, that God had been silent since biblical times? I didn't believe any of those things. It was like the elders had set out a path of dotted lines, and all they asked was for me to fill in the blanks. No wonder the LDS Church was so often quoted as the fastest growing denomination in the world.

It was hard to remain neutral, to keep all this on an intellectual level. But these were serious issues that would cause any sincere Christian to struggle. As with exaltation, I wasn't entirely comfortable with other aspects of their doctrine, especially the temple.

Mormon temples are sacred places where holy rites called ordinances take place, and nonmembers are not allowed to participate. The elders said they could not reveal specifics of temple rituals, but they could talk about them in general terms. "Sacred not secret" was the mantra they repeated. Again, this made sense.

If something is important to me personally, I don't go around telling everyone about it.

Yet, at the same time, the temple scared me. It repre-sented the unknown—the variable that could change the entire equation. I read as much as I could about it online. Sticking to academic sources wasn't easy, but I managed.

"So you can't discuss temple rituals with me," I said at one of my lessons with the elders, "but can you talk about them with each other?"

Elder Luke shook his head.

The temple was so special that what happened there could not be discussed outside its walls, even among believers. I was stepping in deep water, and I couldn't see the bottom. I wasn't allowed to view it from the shore either. Before I could go further, the elders expected me to paddle out to sea.

* * *

My time with the elders was a lot different than how I had studied religion in the past. Besides the convenience of teachers coming into my living room, they had a fixed interest in what I accepted as true.

Unlike my former college professors, who tried to remain neutral in such matters, the missionaries were candid with how they felt about God. They believed in their church, and they wanted me to believe in it too.

Many times during our talks, I could practically feel their conviction. It poured out in their voices, and I could see it in their eyes. At times, it was almost tangible and made what they said easier to believe. They already talked about things that were important to me like Jesus Christ, the Holy Spirit, and following God's plan.

My resolve to stay neutral melted away, and I could

feel it slipping out of reach. The last time I had learned about God with such an open heart was when I was a child.

So often as adults, we approach the Bible with preconceived notions. We question things that are hard to believe and demand proof after proof. If the evidence isn't up to our liking, we dismiss it and move on. As a boy, I wasn't half as cynical.

Back then, my mother sent me to catechism at St. Mary's parochial school. It was probably one-tenth of a mile from Lincoln Elementary, the public school I attended during the day. Most Monday nights, I would walk to catechism by myself, and it was a real treat. I had never felt so independent before.

Sometimes I would walk there with a friend and his mother, but that was fine because it was by choice. No one made me do it. My friend's name was Guy, and he wanted to be a comedian one day, so he'd use the time to try out his latest jokes.

The entire trek took maybe five minutes, but as a kid, I imagined I was on a long journey. In between Guy's comedy, a bully could ambush us or a vicious dog could attack, but I wasn't scared. I had my backpack, and I wasn't afraid to swing it. No doubt my math book could do some real damage. It had hurt my own brain often enough.

Inevitably, I wound up in a classroom with a group of other kids and a nun who was our teacher. I didn't think she was a very good nun because she didn't wear a wimple. All that best nuns wore wimples and could fly like Sally Fields. Everyone knew that.

I can't remember the woman's name so I'll just call her Sister Ruth. She was a thin lady with glasses and short gray hair. She always wore dark colors, either black or a deep blue, with a small cross around her neck.

Sister Ruth would tell stories about Jesus and read from a children's Bible complete with lifelike pictures of the Savior. I once thought this illustrated book was the one true Bible from which all others derived. A nun used it, after all. What else was I to think?

One day, Sister Ruth was telling us about the Ten Commandments. I had already heard about them from my mother, but Ruth mentioned one I didn't recall. It was called adultery.

"Isn't that against the law?" I asked.

"The Ten Commandments are laws," Sister Ruth said.

"But isn't it against the law of the United States? Don't people go to jail for that?"

"Dan," she said, "what's more important: the laws of God or the laws of the United States?"

"The laws of God, of course." *Especially when you're talking to a nun*, I thought.

"It's a good thing you understand that," Sister Ruth said. "Some people never do. Now, let's continue."

Like the elders, Sister Ruth didn't just tell me about God. Her words weren't for simple information, to broaden my world view, or present one side to a story. She wanted me to absorb the lesson, to believe it in a way that would command real change. She provided concrete answers about God and his teachings.

But even at that age, I never took what teachers said as gospel. It was something I learned from my mother. When I got home from catechism, she would ask what Sister Ruth had taught, and her answers didn't always match up.

"We learned about how Jesus turned water into wine.

This statue at a cemetery in Augusta depicts
St. Joseph holding the baby Jesus. Augusta has
a rich Catholic tradition.

It was his first miracle!" I said.

"That's very true. Jesus did many miracles," my mother might say.

To her, loving the Savior and recognizing his power was paramount. Jesus was born of the Virgin Mary, died on the cross for our sins, and was resurrected on the third day. That was the core of what made us Catholic. Period. The end.

Back then I assumed the whole world believed as we did. I had never heard of another church or another way. Everyone believed in and accepted Jesus as the truth.

But some issues were fine to question. For example, my mother didn't like going to confession. "Priests are just men like everyone else. Confess your sins to God," she would say.

It sounded like a decent plan, so that's what I did too. In a strange way, my mother taught me to have faith but question the church; to believe in Christ but not what everyone said about him, even if that person was quoting the Bible. She wanted me to see God with both my heart and my head. The problem was that they rarely agreed.

Other memories from catechism gained new relevance too. While reading the Bible with Sister Ruth, I distinctly recalled Jesus mentioning "other sheep" that he had to bring into the flock. It sounded so mysterious, but when I asked about it, Sister Ruth could not provide an answer. It was a mystery, but one the Book of Mormon solved. In it, the Latter-day Saints believe Jesus visited America. The concept sounds crazy, but I could not deny that the Bible left the possibility open. When I pointed that out, the elders were all too pleased.

I had read somewhere that converting to a new faith was like falling in love. That metaphor never meant so much to me as it did during that time. It wasn't just a comparison or touching quote; it was something that was happening to me a little at a time. The elders' belief that God would speak to my heart and provide a personal revelation of the truth of their gospel was beautiful.

I loved God, and I wanted to know what his plan was for me. According to the elders, I didn't have to wonder anymore. I could see myself as a member of the Church. I could start a whole new life surrounded by people of principle. I could be closer to the Lord than ever before. I wanted it so much.

Maybe too much.

What had started as academic curiosity and research for an article had evolved into something personal. Something that could change my life . . . if I let it.

But I couldn't let my feelings get the best of me. I needed some perspective, and for that, I turned to the one place that always helped me feel close to God: St. Mary's.

It was the most beautiful church in Augusta. Of course, I was biased, but that wasn't the only reason I felt that way. The building had classic appeal, like a touch of the Middle Ages in the heart of modern times. With its stone facade and triple-arched doors, it reminded me of a castle. The inside was my favorite part. Pews filled the arcade, leading up to a white altar framed by angels. From the back of the room, it always looked so far away, as if I were gazing at a vision just over the horizon, at a promise barely out of reach.

Stained glass windows lined the walls, bending the sunlight into radiant hues of red and blue. Each window depicted a scene from the Bible. From the birth of Christ to the Resurrection, it was all rendered here in vibrant color for everyone to enjoy. The windows at St. Mary's challenged me to look beyond the visible, to see beyond the temporary, to ponder where I was now and where I hoped to be.

That Sunday, I sat next to the window of Jesus as a boy, teaching in the temple. Mary was in the background draped in blue. I wondered what the real Mary had been thinking at that moment, what had gone through her mind as she watched her son. It's always been uncertain to me how much Mary knew, but her faith was clear. Even if she did not understand God's plan, she was ready to follow it through.

I wanted faith like Mary's, and I had it staring me in the eye in the form of the elders. They offered what I wanted. Why didn't I take it?

After Mass, I prayed in the pew hoping for an answer. None came. People lingered for a while and chatted in small groups. No one talked to me the way people would in the LDS Church. St. Mary's was more about quiet reflection than community. Ironically, I never felt alone at St. Mary's. It was too familiar. It was home.

People shuffled out of the building a few at a time until I was the only person left. If this were a movie, the priest would have found his way over to me. Instead, he ducked into a small room beside the pulpit. All was quiet, and the silence offered a special kind of peace.

I walked over to where the priest had gone and knocked on the door. He was gathering hymnbooks into piles and raised his head to look at me. He was a tall, sturdy man in his late fifties or so, with brown hair and big glasses. I didn't know his name. I just knew his collar.

"Father," I said, "can I speak with you for a minute?"

"Of course," he said. Coming out of the room, he motioned me over to the nearest pew. "Is there something I can help you with?"

I didn't know where to begin. When you have a complex problem, it's hard to get people to listen—really listen—and that's what I needed. I needed advice from someone who loved the Lord like I did.

"Father, this might sound weird, but I've met some missionaries from the LDS Church. I never thought I'd believe what they say, but lately I've been feeling like it might be true."

"There's room for everyone at God's table," he said. I scanned his eyes for anger but could find none. He waited for me to say something more.

"Father, part of me thinks it would be good to join their church, but they have secrets they can't share with people outside their faith. It scares me. I don't want to give up on our church for something I'm not allowed to know."

"Maybe you don't come to church every Sunday, but it sounds like you have always been Catholic in your heart," he said. "If that's the case, perhaps you shouldn't rush into things. You don't have to make your mind up today or even this week. If it's the right thing to do now, it will be the right thing to do later, won't it?"

"I guess."

"Then think about it more, and make your decision once you're ready. I have somewhere to be, but you can call me at the rectory office if you would like to discuss this further," he said.

"Thank you for your time."

He smiled and left me in the pew. It was true. I didn't have to decide right now, but I wondered if I'd ever make up my mind. When in doubt, stall. It sounded like good advice to me.

6.

A CRACK IN THE MORTAR

I COULDN'T FIGURE OUT WHAT Elder Luke was doing.

When the waitress set our dessert down, he snatched a cup of strawberry sauce and poured it onto an empty plate. We were sitting in a booth at the Ground Round, a restaurant known for everything from burgers to nachos and quesadillas. The latest Top-40 song played in the background as Luke hunched over the table.

A row of powdered pastries sat on a plate between us. He took one and bit a hole into one end. Then, with eyes fixed in deep concentration, he grabbed a spoon and scooped sauce off his plate and dribbled it into the confection's hollow center. He did this repeatedly in silence; so many times, in fact, that I felt mesmerized by the action.

Finally I asked, "What are you doing?"

"Filling it," he said.

Eventually the strawberry sauce trickled out of the corners of the pastry, and Elder Luke sank the dessert into his mouth.

I enjoyed seeing him at times like these when he was a person instead of a missionary. He took his calling so seriously, and though we shared dozens of conversations,

I wasn't any closer to understanding him than the day we first met.

At least eating was an equalizer. It was the one time when the elders and I could leave our roles aside and be people. We weren't teachers and students at the dinner table. We were friends.

Elder Childs must have been especially hungry that day. When we first arrived at the restaurant, we had to wait on a comfy bench for about five minutes, and I thought he was going to start gnawing on his tie.

"It won't be long," I assured him. Patience is a virtue, or so goes the cliché. It's a hard lesson to swallow when you're starved, apparently, even if you're a missionary. Elder Luke sat with his hands folded in his lap. He peered into the dining room studying whatever was happening inside. I wished I were more like him. In my younger days, I like to think I was.

Nothing ever seemed to bother him, and everything bothered me. Sometimes I felt like a pincushion for opinions. Everyone wanted to drive their perspectives into me like needles, whether it was my family, my boss, or even the elders. With the missionaries though, I didn't mind so much.

Once we had eaten and were onto dessert, Elder Childs had mellowed back into his jovial self. "So did you like the video we showed you the other day?" he asked.

"It was very well done," I said. At the last lesson, we had watched a DVD about the Restoration and Joseph Smith. The production was Hollywood quality and had excellent acting and stunning landscapes. Unlike some other Christian groups, the Mormons really knew how to make a good movie.

When it was over, the elders had stared at me, their eyes as hopeful as ever.

I knew what Elder Childs wanted to hear—that I had felt the Holy Spirit bear testimony of the truth. I had felt comforted, but I didn't tell them that. Just because a story moved my emotions didn't mean it was true. A writer should know that more than most.

I wanted so much to believe, but I didn't want to jump into anything either. Instead, I avoided their questions. It was best not to ponder that moment, even in retrospect. It was better to eat our dessert.

"I've been listening to the CDs you gave me, Elder Luke. Joseph Smith sounds like a riot. He's not what I expected at all," I said. Elder Luke had lent me a lecture from Truman G. Madsen, an LDS professor who studied the life of Joseph Smith. It revealed more of Smith's personal character and habits than I expected. Between praying and miracles, the man liked physical competition.

"He was a person like any of us, Dan," Elder Childs said between chews.

"I wasn't expecting a prophet to be so boisterous. The CD talks about how he loved to wrestle."

"No one could beat him," Elder Luke said. "He used to play this game of strength too. You saw it on the video. It's when two men take a broom handle and sit on the ground facing each other. They both pull on the broom, and whoever is weaker gets lifted into the air."

"Really? So, is that what you guys do in your free time?" I asked.

"No," Elder Childs said.

But Luke looked up and stared into the air. "I wonder which one of us would win."

"I'd kill you," Elder Childs said as though it were a matter of fact.

48

I laughed, but neither of them noticed. Childs was too entrenched in his pastry. Luke, on the other hand, pursed his lips. He clearly wanted to test his companion's theory. He may have been a missionary, but he certainly wasn't immune to the jolts of testosterone that come from being a guy. From that day on, I had the impression that he was more competitive than he let on.

When I told my family about my visits with the elders, they were often apathetic. It was the same reaction I got when I tried to discuss the X-Men. Other people, however, got angry, and I discovered that some people considered being rude to the elders a badge of honor. Those reactions only made me more sympathetic to Luke and Childs. One of the more memorable responses I personally witnessed happened during a blind date. A friend from high school had set me up, so one Friday night I found myself at a local restaurant making conversation with a girl I just met. The conversation was pleasant enough until she asked what church I attended. I told her I was Catholic but had recently been visiting with the Mormons.

Her jaw fell open, and the slice of steak she had just carved tilted on her fork, like a seesaw that had gained weight on one side. It was like something out of *Seinfeld*. She later apologized and described the Mormons as "really weird." I told her I understood because some of what they did was strange to me too.

Around that time the elders taught me about a practice called fast and testimony meeting. On the first Sunday of every month LDS Church members fast for twenty-four hours. The elders invited me to try it, and I agreed. Elder Childs was glad with my attempt until he realized something went wrong in our communication.

"How did you manage with the fast?" he asked. "The hardest part for me is not drinking."

"I didn't realize you couldn't drink anything," I confessed. "I guzzled orange juice all day."

"Oh no! I guess we didn't explain it right," he said.

I started to realize that the missionaries were giving me little assignments: read the Book of Mormon, pray, fast. None of what they requested was very difficult. I wanted to see how the Mormons lived, and besides, if it made the elders happy, what harm could it do?

* * *

"It's very important to keep the Sabbath day holy," Elder Luke said at the end our next lesson. "We don't spend money on Sunday."

"What do you do all day?" I asked.

"You can watch a movie as long as it's wholesome. You might take a nap. Sometimes that's what I do."

I must have looked old to Luke if he thought I needed a nap. I found a certain comedy in the moment: a twenty-year-old suggesting I sleep in my spare time. Talk about a party.

I never understood what super religious people did for fun. Elder Childs said he liked to go boating sometimes, but since I was a few grand short of a sailboat, that wasn't an option.

"Do you have any other questions?" Elder Childs asked. "We have another appointment soon."

"Yes," I said.

I had printed some articles from an online encyclopedia and wanted their opinions. A few choice passages had caught my attention. "This article says adult members of the Church receive a garment that they wear underneath clothing. What exactly does that mean?"

"Pretty much what it said," Elder Childs commented.

I hoped he would elaborate, but instead he turned to Luke.

Taking a breath, Luke reached into his jacket. "If it's in this book, we can talk about it," he said. Luke plucked a small white volume from his pocket and flipped through its pages.

"What's that?" I asked.

"It outlines rules we have to follow," Elder Luke said.

My toes had touched rogue territory again. Only this time it felt more serious than an accidental lock of my car door.

Elder Childs stared at Luke as his companion turned the pages, and I got the feeling he was avoiding my eyes. Whenever I had a hard question, I usually turned to him for the answer. Where Elder Luke sounded so official, Childs put it into familiar terms. This time, I guess, that wouldn't work.

Luke found the passage he needed and cited that temple garments were given to members after they visited the temple. The garments were worn on a daily basis and served as a constant reminder of covenants with God.

The journalist in me rejoiced. What a fascinating practice!

"You're wearing them now?" I asked.

Luke nodded.

"Can I see what they look like?"

He pulled his jacket closed. "We're taught to be modest."

At the time, I hadn't realized what I was asking. I didn't mean for him to undress. I just wanted to see a piece of the garment, a sleeve, a collar, anything.

"Dan, this is sort of a sensitive issue for us," Elder Childs said.

"I understand, but I like learning about your culture."

Elder Luke looked at his watch. "We should probably get going. We'll see you another time."

We exchanged our good-byes, shook hands, and I walked them to the door. I had heard whispers of special Mormon clothes but never believed them. The elders had worn something unique all this time, and I never knew it. There was still so much more to learn about their faith. The student in me was thrilled.

But I was more than a student now, and that realization struck me like a hard punch to the gut. This wasn't a college class. This wasn't a bonus question on a test.

This was my life.

I had thought of converting when I didn't know I'd have to wear special clothes every day. Every single day. It was a pretty big obligation, and the elders had never mentioned it. Not once. When were they going to tell me? Or did they plan to tell me at all?

That night, I could barely sleep. I felt so naïve and disgusted with myself. The garments themselves weren't the issue. Jewish people wore special hats; some monks wore special shirts underneath their frocks. It wasn't unheard of to wear special clothes, but if the elders didn't tell me about this, what else might jump out after baptism? What weren't they telling me?

Those questions kept me awake. Each one was a hot cattle prod that stung worse than the last. Had the elders lied to me this whole time? Did they care about me at all, or was I just another convert, a trophy to win for their church?

I wrestled with my blanket well into the night and punched my pillow several times, but no matter how hard I hit it, I didn't feel better.

The next morning I went to my sister's house for breakfast. She stood in front of her stove, wearing a frumpy pink bathrobe. Her hair, still wet from the shower, was swept up into a towel that was folded into a makeshift turban. She hummed to herself as she beat some eggs with a whisk.

"What's wrong?" she asked. Sunlight shone through a window beside her, and the bright yellow walls of her kitchen magnified its glow.

"Why?"

"You're usually more talkative."

I debated whether to tell her anything. I had told her about the missionaries before, and she always stayed on the fence. She was happy I liked them but not happy enough to meet them herself.

But I needed someone to talk to, so I confided what was on my mind—conversion, my visit with the priest, discovering the garments. I felt stupid. Men my age had problems with women and booze. They stayed out too late and partied too much. Me? I had trouble with Mormons.

When I was finished sharing my thoughts, my sister set a plate of scrambled eggs in front of me. For a moment, I thought, it resembled my brain. Long ago, she had adopted a philosophy from our mother: food makes any situation better.

"You might not want to hear this," she said. "I know you think these missionaries are your friends. Maybe they are, but they come because they want another church member, not because they like you. You might have forgotten why they visit, but they haven't."

She patted me on the shoulder and turned back to the stove.

I didn't want it to be true, but maybe it was. The elders may have liked my company, but that was secondary to everything else. Conversion was their goal, and it would guide anything they did, from the smallest decision to the largest, including what they revealed about their church. Including what they revealed to me.

* * *

I kept thinking about those mysterious temple garments and how close I had come to needing them myself.

All those times I went to church, and I never knew what was going on. Everyone who spoke to me, everyone who had shaken my hand were all taking part in this practice, and they expected me to take part in it one day too.

I couldn't let my feelings linger in limbo. Whatever the elders' reaction might be, I had to be honest. There would be no secrets. At least not on my end.

The next time the missionaries came, they took their usual spots on my sofa. I sat in my recliner and leaned in with my elbows on my knees. "Before we begin, there's something I need to tell you."

"All right," Elder Luke said. The Book of Mormon was already in his lap.

"After you two left, I was upset about the garments. I want you to understand that the garments themselves aren't the issue. It bothers me that you never mentioned them."

Emotion erupted in my voice. I couldn't hide it. I've never been good at that. In that way, I was jealous of Elder Luke. Elder Childs' forehead wrinkled in concern, but to Luke, it looked like I had made a mundane remark.

"I've been truthful with you about my intention to learn about this church. Now I feel like you can't even be honest with me," I said.

"We would never lie to you, Dan," Elder Childs told me.

Luke opened his Book of Mormon and began to study whatever passage he found inside. I expected him to share something insightful, but he didn't.

"I'm trying to see things from your point of view," Elder Childs said. "I really am. I understand why you would be concerned."

"I think we should get on with the lesson we have planned," Elder Luke interjected. "If we turn to page—"

Elder Childs reached for his Book of Mormon, and after a minute, so did I. I don't remember what our lesson was that day. I had a hard time paying attention. The elders went on as if I had said nothing at all. I wanted them to convince me that they had good reason to keep their secrets.

Perhaps I wanted too much.

"We'd like to bring a member of our church to our next lesson," Elder Childs said when he and Luke were getting ready to leave. "We'd like you to become friends with some local members of the ward."

"Fine," I said.

Only it wasn't.

A crack had formed in the mortar of the friendship I shared with the elders, and they had nothing to say about it. No cure for my concern. No solution. Only silence.

7.

TRANSFERS

THE NEXT DAY I GOT Chinese food from a local takeout place called Canton Express. It was one of several shops clustered near an old graveyard on Bangor Street. I often drove by the cemetery, but it was the first time I ever saw it up close. While waiting for my order, I decided to take a stroll.

The cold had let up a little. It might have been in the mid-twenties or so, and to my thick Maine bones, it nearly felt like spring. Indeed, warmer weather was about a month away. It was March now, and I had been seeing the missionaries since the beginning of January. I saw them so often that it was strange to go more than a few days without their company. I thought we were friends, but to them maybe it *was* just a façade, a mission mandate, or another rule to follow.

Snow covered the earth in a thick cushion that crunched beneath my feet, leaving the imprint of my winter boots behind in a trail that led to me. Most of the tombstones were hidden beneath winter's white surface, but a few of the larger ones poked into view. In time, the snow would be gone, and the ground would see daylight again. The land would show for what it really was, not just what it looked like right now.

I came to a small monument that displayed a family name. "Haskell," it read. It stuck out of the snow in a carved shape that reminded me of a pawn in chess. I wondered what the Haskells believed about God. It might be morbid to think, but one day, I would end up beneath a stone with dates that marked the years of my life. Yet every moment brings me a little closer to God. When I think of it that way, it's not so bad.

Maybe that was the main purpose of faith—to provide solace. Sometimes the elders would say they knew certain things were true. They knew Joseph Smith was a prophet of God. They knew their church was true.

I didn't know that, but I wanted the kind of faith that would perfect my life and make me the man I wanted to be. I wanted to say either the Catholic Church or the LDS Church was true, and I wanted to feel that truth in every fiber of my being. No doubts. No questions. I wanted them erased like chalk from a board. Instead, it felt like my doubts were etched in permanent ink.

Maybe God had another plan for my life, and meeting the elders was just another step to get there. A stepping stone, not a destination.

It may have been time to ask the missionaries not to return, to cut our connection for good. But I didn't want to do that. I had promised myself I'd be good to the elders. It was a promise I intended to keep.

I wouldn't close the door to conversion, but it wasn't wide open either. Instead, I'd leave it open just a crack, enough for a miracle, and pray for an answer, whatever it may be.

* * *

I set an extra chair out for the visiting ward member over my next few missionary visits. He never came.

"He had a family emergency. Things come up, but he'll be here next time," Elder Childs had said at the man's first absence.

"Fine," I told him.

Except that the ward member canceled a second and third time as well. Elder Childs didn't look too happy about it, but it was apparently his job to relay each excuse to me. They all consisted of vague family emergencies.

I didn't press the issue, and if I had to guess, Elder Childs was glad I didn't. While his words were always apologetic, I could sense his irritation. A hint of disappointment was in his eyes. He may have tried to hide it, but I could tell anyway. At least his emotions were sincere even if the ward member's intentions were not.

After the third excuse, the elders never mentioned the man again. We all pretended like nothing happened. It was disappointing, I'll admit. The missionaries wouldn't stay forever, and once they left, my strongest connection to the Church would be broken.

Maybe that's what God wanted.

Transfers came a week later. That's when the elders relocate to a new area if the mission president deems it necessary. I called the missionaries to check on the news. Elder Childs answered the phone.

"I called to see what was happening," I said.

"Well, Elder Luke will be staying, and I'll be moving to a new area," he told me.

It felt like a balloon had popped. Transfers happened the next day. I'd probably never see Elder Childs again.

"I'd wish you luck, but I know you won't need it," I said. "It was a real pleasure getting to know you."

"It was a pleasure to meet you as well, Dan."

"Don't tell Elder Luke I said this, but you were my favorite."

I could sense a smile on the other end of the phone.

"Good-bye, Elder Childs."

"Good-bye, Dan."

Several days passed before I contacted the missionaries again. Whoever the new guy was, I was worried about him. Elder Luke and Elder Childs had gotten along like brothers, and I doubted anyone could match the camaraderie they shared. Not only that, but making someone feel welcome didn't hit me as one of Elder Luke's skills. During our initial interview for the paper, he had confessed that transfers were his least favorite part of the mission.

Now it was something we had in common.

I called him early one morning to leave a message of encouragement. I was ready to leave a voicemail when, to my surprise, he answered the phone. He sounded winded as if he had been running.

"Good morning, Elder Luke. This is Dan Harrington," I said.

"Good morning."

"Are you all right? You're breathing heavy."

"I'm exercising," he said.

"I wanted to check up on you and see how my elder is doing."

"I'm fine."

He didn't sound like he wanted to talk, but did he ever? As usual, it was up to me to charge ahead.

"Elder Luke, I wanted to make sure you knew that even though Elder Childs and I got along really well, I think of you as my friend too. I hope that's how you think of me."

*In a post-mission visit, Elder Childs returned to his
Augusta stomping grounds, which included his old spot
on my couch where we discussed LDS beliefs.*

"Yes, I certainly do," he said.

There was silence then, but not the usual kind. This
wasn't specific to Elder Luke. It was the kind of pause that
happens when men get too close to sharing their feelings.

"We're having a baptism tomorrow," Elder Luke said
finally. "You're welcome to come."

"I'll be there."

* * *

As usual, I arrived at the church a few minutes late.
I always operate under the assumption that it takes five
minutes to reach any destination as long as I hurry. I
parked my car and dashed inside.

Elder Luke was talking with two men in the hallway.
One of them was a ward member I recognized, but the
other was someone I had never seen. He was a tall man
in his mid-twenties and was dressed in a long white tunic
that reminded me of a hospital robe.

Elder Luke's attire stood out even more. He was dressed all in white from his shoes to his shirt and tie. Even his belt. It reminded me of an angel. Perhaps that was the point.

I wanted to stare, but the trio turned to greet me as I approached.

"Dan, this is Roger. This is his baptism," Elder Luke said.

The young man offered his hand with a smile.

I tried to think of something appropriate to say. "Congratulations," I said.

"Thank you," he responded.

"Excuse me, gentlemen. I'll let you do your stuff," I said. I patted Elder Luke on the back before I continued down the hall.

Twenty or so ward members were congregated in a classroom with a piano and a television. The space must have been used for primary school because the alphabet was posted along the wall, and children's books were stacked in colored crates on the floor.

I spotted the new elder right away. He sat on the end of one row, by himself, dressed in standard mission garb. His hair was a fiery shade of red, which made him stand out even more. The color made me think of Richie Cunningham from *Happy Days*. Seeing him evoked a sad feeling too. The new missionary meant Elder Childs was gone for good—the end of an era.

After a deep breath, I went over to introduce myself.

"Hello, I'm Dan. I'm one of Elder Luke's investigators," I said.

"It's nice to meet you. I'm Elder Allred."

"I appreciate your service, and I hope you like it here, Elder."

"Thank you."

I pulled a chair up behind him, and my mind went blank. That was all I could think of to say. He nodded and then went back to staring toward the front of the room.

Maybe making someone feel welcome wasn't on my list of talents after all.

I had been to a baptism before, but I had never seen Elder Luke get in the water. The font was in a small opening at the head of the room, and a tilted mirror mounted on the wall allowed everyone to see what was happening. The two men entered the font from a set of stairs, and they stood in the water together. Roger was at least a foot taller than Luke, so the baptism required him to fall completely on his back in order to be immersed.

After he came up from of the water, there was some discussion that I could barely hear. It sounded like a murmur from where I sat, but they redid the ceremony, dunking Roger a second time.

When the two men stepped out of the font, the lights dimmed, and we watched a video about the importance of baptism. Twenty minutes later, the lights came on and Roger re-entered the room dressed in khakis and a button down shirt. People shook his hand and patted his back in congratulations, a welcome into the ward family.

That could have been me.

It could have been my baptism. But once the ceremony was over, everyone would go home, and years down the line, when the elders were just a memory, who of the ward would stand with me? Certainly not the guy who was too busy to make it to one of my lessons.

People filed out of the room a few at a time, and Elder Allred collected the folding chairs and put them in the corner. Luke returned, now dressed in his usual mission attire, and retreated to the piano, where he started to play. A voice caught my attention as I made my way over to him.

"I saw your story about us," someone said. It was Jon, a member of the ward. He was about six feet tall and a few years older than I was. He wore glasses and a friendly smile. Jon spoke to me often at church, and we probably would have become good friends if our lives weren't so different. He was married with several young children. Though he would never admit it, I knew he was a pillar of the local ward.

"Are we starting to grow on you?" he asked.

"You could say that," I said.

"You might have to be careful. Usually when we're in the paper, someone from another denomination writes a nasty letter about us."

"That kind of attitude comes from people who don't know you."

"It can be intimidating going to a new church."

"True," I said. Sometimes I was still intimidated when I visited his.

Elder Luke played a reverent tune on the piano. He didn't acknowledge us as we approached.

"You know, some people are surprised we have electricity," Jon said. "They think Mormons are like the Amish."

"Oh, those people must have met Elder Luke," I said.

Elder Allred laughed quite loud in the background. It was a good sign. I knew I was going to like him.

Elder Luke cracked a smile, and Jon laughed too.

"Why did Roger have to go into the water twice?" I asked.

Elder Luke stopped playing his music and looked up at me. "His knee didn't go under the water," he explained.

"He was worried about falling back. I guess he didn't trust me."

I wanted to remind Elder Luke that Roger trusted him with the most important thing of all—his faith. I wanted to say that, but I didn't. I was too amazed that Elder Luke had shared how he felt. Some people do it all the time, but for him, it was rare. It meant more than a casual comment. It meant trust.

8.

ADVENTURES DOOR TO DOOR

AROUND THAT TIME, I SET up an interview with the captain of the local chapter of the Salvation Army. Despite the famous Christmas kettles and discount stores, few people were aware that the army was a church, not just a charity. The local pastor was pleased that I wanted to highlight his beliefs in the paper.

His name was Captain Jim Downs. He told me that church members could address him as either captain or pastor. Such an exchange of words was unique among churches, and the captain was certainly an interesting fellow.

Some people joked that he looked like Jesse Ventura, the pro-wrestler and politician. The resemblance wasn't perfect, but it was there. The pastor was a big man, about six feet two, with a shaved head and goatee. He could have easily passed for a bouncer at the local bar if it weren't for his jovial smile and Salvation Army uniform. I had seen him around town on occasion, and he always wore his black suit with red patches on his shoulders that mimicked military garb.

We met at the Salvation Army Church on Pearl Street in Augusta. The building was located in the middle of a neighborhood and would have blended in with the surrounding homes if not for the large, red shield outside its main door.

No pews were inside the church. Instead, chairs were placed in a series of slanted rows that lead to a dais with a podium and large wooden cross. An American flag stood on one side of the dais, and on the other was a red and blue flag that represented the Salvation Army.

As soon as he saw me, the captain rushed out of his office, a small room in the corner, and asked me to sit with him in the main hall. Except for us, the place was empty. He said he liked to keep the building open as late as he could each night in case anyone needed a place to go for help.

During the interview, his cell phone rang several times. He excused himself and took each call. Normally I would have found it irritating, but I didn't blame him. These weren't trivial conversations. Instead, they were from the police and the local homeless shelter.

"I apologize, Dan," he said when he hung up. "A family lost their house in a fire and the shelter is full."

"What will you do?" I asked.

"Probably put them up in a local motel for the night."

Many pastors have told me how much responsibility they carry, but Captain Downs was the only one I saw get calls like that, and it didn't only happen during the hour and a half I spent with him. This was every day. This was the man's life.

When the phone quieted down, he explained that members of the Salvation Army were called Salvationists. "Our church has something called the Articles of War," the captain said. "In it, we declare war on poverty, sickness, and homelessness."

"Is that why you wear an army type uniform, to show that you're at war?"

"Yes, we have a paramilitary-type hierarchy, and we wear these clothes as an outward expression of our Christian faith."

I drew a sharp breath.

"You wear these garments because of your religion?"

"Yes, the uniform makes me visible so people know they can approach me, but everything we do, we do because we're Christian. I wear my uniform almost every day, but initially, I didn't want to wear mine because I didn't want to wear polyester." He laughed.

After an awkward pause, I let out a polite chuckle. It's not that the joke wasn't funny; I just had something else on my mind.

* * *

The next week Elder Luke let me go tracting. That's what the missionaries called going door-to-door looking for people. It was by far the most famous missionary activity, and I wanted to see it up close. It's one thing to read or hear about it but quite another to experience.

A steady rain had washed away what was left of the snow, and it was finally warm enough to leave my winter coat at home. The sky was a dim shade of gray when the elders arrived at my apartment, and the rain had waned to a trickle. I wore a green windbreaker in case the downpour returned. No matter the weather, the elders were determined to spread the good news.

"We wondered if you'd still want to come with us since it was raining," Elder Luke said as he and Allred greeted me.

"I wasn't going to miss this," I told him. "Do you

want to take my car or yours?"

"We're not allowed to have someone in our car. It's one of our rules."

We hadn't even started, and I had already learned a new rule—how educational!

We drove a short distance to one of my least favorite streets in the neighborhood. While a few of the houses looked new, many were rundown. Gaudy lawn ornaments packed some of the front yards with pink flamingos, rusty chairs, and a general assortment of trash. The roof of one small gray house was starting to cave in, and I imagined a wrecking ball exploding it into a million pieces.

We stopped at the home, and Elder Allred knocked on the door. A plastic butterfly the size of a baby hung overhead. If it was supposed to look real, it wasn't doing a very good job. I wondered what the elders thought of the home. Then I felt a spark of guilt. It was wrong of me to judge.

An elderly lady came to the door. She was heavyset with short gray hair and squinted at us as if we were far away.

"How are you doing today, ma'am?" Elder Allred asked with a smile.

"Oh, I could be better," she said.

"Why's that?"

The lady told us how her friend was sick, and she was worried about her.

"That's too bad. We hope she gets better," Elder Allred said.

"She probably won't. She's very old."

"Well, we can hope for the best. You know, when some people are sick, they think more about God." That was the transition. From then on, the conversation was about religion. The woman kept squinting at the elders, going back and forth, as each one talked.

"We'd love to come and talk to you more about this. Would it be all right for us to come back?" Elder Allred asked.

"Oh, I don't know," she said, shaking her head.

"We'd be available Tuesday or Wednesday."

"Those aren't good days for me."

"Thursday would also work for us."

"I'm busy Thursdays."

"Busy, busy," Elder Allred said. He presented her with a card. "You can call us if you would like, or we could call you."

She hesitated a moment. "I don't like to give out my number."

"Well, call us if you have any questions."

She took the card, and we bid her farewell.

Elder Luke knocked on another door, where a young mother lived. From the window, I could see a baby sitting in her lap. Light from a TV screen flickered across their faces. She got up from her recliner and peeked out the door.

"Hello," Elder Luke said.

Without a word, the woman turned around and plopped herself back in front of the television, adjusting the baby. We stood at the door for a moment. She raised an arm as if to swat a fly. "I'm all set!" Venom was in her tone.

"Thank you," Elder Luke said.

"I'm all set!" she screamed. Of all the things she would teach her child, I doubted manners would be one of them.

At the next house, a lady with big glasses that reminded

me of Velma from Scooby-Doo, was much easier to deal with.

"Oh, the Mormons," she said. "I know all about you! I love your commercials. They're so touching." She had limped over to meet us at the door and began to say how her leg had been hurt during a bad fall.

As the missionaries expressed concern for her injury, a cat pranced over and pressed itself against the woman's ankle. She scooped it up and hugged it close to her face. Her eyes locked on the feline, and it squinted back in approval. Elder Luke asked about the pet, and this propelled the woman into a long-winded story that zigzagged from the cat to her house to her family. Just when I thought I'd hear stories about her husband for the rest of my life, Elder Luke asked if she would be interested in going to church.

"No, thank you. That's not necessary; I've seen your commercials already. I do enjoy them," she said.

Elder Allred said something more, but the lady was too busy cuddling her cat to notice. The pet was happy with all the attention, and its purring grew more fervent. The lady thanked us one final time for the uplifting commercials and retreated into her living room.

We proceeded to one of the newest homes on the street. It was a two-story house with new yellow siding. The driveway was shaped like a crescent moon, and the lawn was neatly mowed. As soon as Elder Allred knocked on the door, a man poked his head from a second-story window.

"Hello, can I help you?" he said. It reminded me of *The Wizard of Oz* when Dorothy gets to the Emerald City and the doorman pops his head out to greet them.

Elder Luke said something to the man, but I don't

recall what. I was half expecting the guy to spit on us and was getting ready to jump out of the way. This was Augusta, Maine, not Oz, after all. Too bad.

"I'll be right down," the man said.

I nearly joked that he went to get a gun, but I didn't want to worry the elders. This was serious business for them. Luke waited with his usual Spock-like stare at the door, paying no heed to me, but Allred smiled when I explained my *Wizard of Oz* analogy.

Moments later the man joined us outside. He was slightly taller than any of us and sported the type of muscle that comes from hard labor. He wore a black tank top, and his arms were built to an impressive size. He must have been in his forties and had short salt and pepper hair, a dark tan, and a goatee. I guessed that he worked in construction, and he told us he was a maintenance man.

"Thanks for coming, guys, but I know the Lord. I love Jesus," he said. "Have you ever heard of the mountain men?"

We shook our heads.

"It's a gang of bikers I used to run with. Back then, I did drugs and got in fistfights. Man, I used to crack some heads. We did some pretty awful stuff. I didn't believe in God, but I learned in war, when bullets are flying, there aren't any atheists. When people need help, the first thing they do is look to God."

His words made sense except for the cracking heads part. As the man continued in his story of conversion, I glanced over to Elder Luke. His stare was in full throttle, and it came in handy at times like these. He just looked and listened, though I suspected he was waiting for the perfect time to intercept the man with some words about Joseph Smith Jr.

"You know what I don't like about the Catholic Church," the man told us. "It's the way you have to say 'forgive me, father, for I have sinned.' You don't need to confess your sins to anyone but God."

Elder Allred nodded in agreement, so the man started to confess his sins. They mostly involved beating people up but also promiscuity. I've always found it ironic that Protestants view confession as a major point of conflict when they often seek absolution from pastors, strangers, or in this case, elders. The sacrament of confession just took these conversations a step further.

"So thanks, guys, thanks." The man concluded his monologue of crimes. "But if God wanted me to join your faith, He'd let me know."

We shook his hand again, and after we left, I turned to Elder Luke. "Why didn't you try to convince that guy to come to church?"

"Some people are just blind," Luke said. "He said he wanted a sign, but we were right there in front of him."

"What were you thinking when he was talking about all the fights he had been in?"

"He was thinking that he could take that guy down," Elder Allred said.

We all got a good laugh, but Elder Luke didn't argue with his companion's assessment.

In a strange way, the biker had reminded me of Sister Ruth. One day in catechism, she wore a stern expression, the kind adults had when they were about to say something serious. My grade school teacher had taken such a look when she explained the importance of stop, drop, and roll. In her own way, I suppose, Sister Ruth was about to address a spiritual fire, and not the good kind.

My classmates must have sensed it too because the

room grew quiet. Even the kids who whispered in the back row had little to say. Sister Ruth looked at each of us, her eyes honed like a laser on our souls.

"Some people," she said, "think it's foolish to believe in God. They'll tell you he isn't there or that we don't need him. But what do these same people do when someone in their family is sick or they're in really bad trouble?"

She paused. The effect was dramatic enough for me to remember all these years later.

"They pray," she said. "They look to God for help and comfort. But how do you feel when someone comes to you only when they want to get something out of you? People of faith don't just seek God when they think they need him. A person with real faith knows he needs God every single day."

Of all the lessons I learned from Sister Ruth, that one may have been the most powerful. God didn't want us to think about him occasionally. Religion wasn't something we did out of convenience or in our leisure. Real faith meant relying on Christ all the time.

I think that's the heart of humility—recognizing where your blessings come from and realizing who the true master is. It's one of those lessons that's easier to preach than it is to live, but I try.

9.

MOTHER'S DAY

THE LAST TIME I SAW Elder Luke was on Mother's Day 2007. I arrived at church five minutes late, as usual. On the way there, every light had turned red and every slow-poke in town found a reason to drive in front of me. It must have been the work of Satan. Still, I persevered and arrived at 9:05.

I dashed into the church and ducked into my favorite place, the overflow. The main hall bustled with people, many more than usual. One lady greeted me with a smile.

"You've become a regular," she whispered.

"I guess so."

The elders sat in the pulpit at the front of the room. Elder Allred smiled at me with a nod, but Elder Luke stared straight ahead, concentrating on nothing in particular.

A speaker noted how it was Mother's Day and that the elders would give us their thoughts on the subject.

Elder Allred took the stage first. In private, he had confessed that he hated giving speeches. Talking in front of a large crowd made him nervous, but I don't think he gave himself enough credit. He stood tall behind the podium, shoulders back and head high with confidence.

"Since I started my mission, I've missed my mother's cooking," he began. "Elder Luke tries, but it's not quite the same."

Everyone laughed, especially me.

"Seriously, one of the first things I remember my mother teaching me was how to tie my shoes. It sounds like a simple thing, but it is very important. Every morning when I wake up, I have to tie my shoes. Little things like this help me on my mission," he said.

He went on to talk of Mary, quoting scriptures of how Jesus, just before his death, wanted to make sure that his own mother would be all right. I was familiar with that passage in the Bible and appreciated the insight.

When Elder Allred finished his speech, Luke adjusted his suit jacket and took his place behind the podium. He told us how, while tracting with Allred, they had come upon a house with an old RV parked out front. Two adults were cleaning it out. When the missionaries had approached, a lady told them that her children were cleaning the RV as a Mother's Day gift. "I wish every day was Mother's Day," the woman had said.

Luke paused in his tale and gazed at the ward. "I ask you, is this woman any less a mother the next day? Or the next?" he said. "Why should our acts of kindness end the day after Mother's Day?" He went on to testify that he had gained much of his faith from his parents, and that he was grateful to know God and to be a member of this church.

As he spoke, the strangest thing happened. Emotion crept into his voice. For a moment, it faltered, and I thought he might break down. But he didn't.

Luke was far too subtle for that. In fact, most people in the audience might not have noticed, but I did. I saw more in Elder Luke that day than I had in most of our lessons.

As I listened to him speak of his mother, I realized that he was someone I respected, someone I was proud to know. God had something wonderful planned for Elder Luke, and I wished I could be there to see it.

But I wouldn't be. That much I knew. All too often, life is like that.

People come in, make their mark, and leave. It's doesn't matter if they're a missionary or not. In recording these events, I wonder if that's why writing has always meant so much to me. In a changing world where people disappear like smoke in the wind, writing can make a moment last. It offers time to ponder and reflect and a chance to hold onto things that possess a special meaning for us.

Transfers came again, and I called the elders to see if they were staying. I had to leave a message, but Elder Allred called back several hours later. He said that Elder Luke was gone and that an Elder Paige had taken his place. I knew I'd never see Luke again. I didn't even get to say good-bye.

I stayed in touch with Elder Allred and continued going to church for another month or so. Allred never sat with me like Luke and Childs did. He and Elder Paige had their own investigators to teach, and I wasn't one of them. It didn't take long for my doubts to take center stage. Every Sunday, people testified to knowing that the Church was true. I wanted to be able to say that, but I couldn't. As much as I liked the idea of a restored gospel, I found myself wondering if certain doctrines really were true.

Slowly I realized that I was a stranger among people who had known each other their whole lives. I didn't belong. So I left. It was as simple as that.

God had answered, and at that point, I was convinced the answer was no.

10

THE MORMONS ARE MISSING

MONTHS PASSED. I CONTINUED writing for the paper, meeting a lot of interesting people, and covering different churches, but no one struck me like the Latter-day Saints. That was largely because of my friendship with the elders. I could visit other congregations several times in a row and never really meet anyone. Sure people would shake my hand and offer a polite greeting, but that's worlds apart from being someone's friend.

I began to think of my time with the elders as my "Mormon Moment." Maybe that's all it was ever meant to be.

Elder Allred had left, and I hadn't gotten to say goodbye to him either, a common motif. It was sort of like an old western where the cowboy rides off into the sunset. Except that instead of a horse, Allred rode a bike. A helmet replaced the cowboy hat, and a name tag stood in for the sheriff's star. It was a fun image to play with.

I spotted the new missionaries around town a few times but never talked to them. They dressed like the elders I knew, had the same look, held the same book, but were strangers. Maybe it was better that way. What all the missionaries did, in the end, was leave. But I was grateful for the elders I knew. They gave me a taste of another life, a glimpse of another faith, and a new view of fellowship to ponder.

Eventually, I began bumping into ward members in public. At the grocery store or at the gas station, there they were. Then the bishop started going to my gym. We'd make small talk at the workout machines before going our separate ways. It made me miss the Church.

Then one Sunday in October, a miracle happened. I woke up early. No alarm. No loud bird at the window. No crazy neighbor mowing his lawn at dawn. I simply awoke and felt rested.

It's an uncommon occurrence for me. Night is one of my favorite times to write, and it can be hard to pry myself away from a story. I'm sure I'm not the only person who cheats himself out of sleep either. For some reason, most people today are under the impression that laptops, cell phones, and iPods are more important than a good night's rest.

On most mornings the alarm had to yank me from sleep like a deep-sea fisherman wrestling a shark from the water. Not exactly a pleasant experience. On those precious days when I woke naturally on my own, few things felt as sweet against my skin as sunshine in the morning.

It was nearly 8:00 a.m. That meant I had plenty of time to get to the LDS church if I wanted. But maybe I shouldn't go. So much time had passed; it might be strange. Bah! I threw the thought aside along with my blanket. It was so early, I could even stay the whole three hours, and not sneak in late like I used to.

I chose a tie, showered, and dressed. I even left on time. Everything was going my way.

That was until I got to the church building. When I

arrived, the parking lot was empty. No one. Not a car in sight.

I checked my watch against the clock on my dash: 8:58. The time was right. Was it Sunday? Yes, I was sure of it. I had yesterday off and had eaten at a restaurant with my family. So where was everyone?

Where were the Mormons?

Had I entered a wrinkle in the space-time continuum, like something out of *Star Trek*? I circled the church twice. All the windows were dark. *Twilight Zone* music began playing in my head.

Perhaps it was the Rapture, and they had all been whisked away to heaven, cars and all. But I was pretty sure there were no vehicles in heaven. At least not ones that ran on dirty, old dinosaur bones.

Maybe the entire congregation was late; their alarm clocks smashed in some sort of hate crime against the Latter-day Saints. In either case, my mind couldn't conjure a lucid scenario.

My parents lived closer to the church than I did, so I stopped at their house to share the unexpected conundrum. My mother and father were in their mid-seventies and in the middle of enjoying breakfast. My father sat in his wheelchair at the kitchen table, sipping from the same cup of coffee that was never far from his lips. It was never enough to drink the beverage either. It always had to be served from that same brown mug. Archie Bunker had his chair. My father had his mug.

My dad had been a firefighter and emergency dispatcher most of his life but not the part that I could remember. My parents had me late in their lives, and my father had retired the year I came into the world. All I remembered of his work was the gold fireman's plaque from the city of Augusta that hung in our living room in honor of his service.

Later in life, my dad lost a leg due to diabetes and a relentless sweet tooth he never thought would be a problem. In fact, some of my earliest memories of my father involved him hiding an assortment of donuts and pastries around the house. Whenever my mother went shopping or on an errand, out the goodies would come. To his credit, he always shared what he had with me.

My mother, meanwhile, stood at the stove, which for her was a workstation but one that she enjoyed. She loved feeding her family and operated as a 24/7 short-order cook ready to prepare a meal at a moment's notice. She was around five feet one, could speak Spanish, and had slight Mexican features that would be hard to place if you didn't know where she was from. For that reason, she liked to joke that she was a mix of Aztec and Mayan, with a splash of Chinese.

My mother had grown up in San Antonio, Texas, and pined for the Lonestar State ever since I was little. The people were friendlier in Texas, the weather better, the grass greener. The list could go on and on and sometimes did.

My parents had met when my father was in the military, and my mother always said that leaving Texas was the worst mistake she ever made.

"Do you want some pancakes?" she asked when she saw me. I still had a key to their home and had let myself in. My mother made the best pancakes in the world, and when I was little, I even called them "pam-ma-cakes." The accent was on the "ma."

"No," I said. "You'll never believe this. The Mormons are missing!"

"What?"

"No one is at the church. I can't believe it!"

"They're probably hiding," my father said. "They're tired of you, and when they saw you coming, they hid. Did you look behind the bushes?"

When I was a young teenager, I had gone through a long phase of being painfully shy. Once I had hidden from some bullies behind a bush. My father never let me live it down.

"The whole congregation can't fit behind some bushes," I told him.

"What about trees? Are there any trees around that church?" he asked with feigned sincerity. He began laughing so hard that he wheezed.

"Don't be silly," my mother said as she turned from the stove. She held a plate of scrambled eggs and set it in front of my father. "They're probably baptizing someone in the river."

My father agreed it was likely scenario. "They're probably at the Kennebec River right now. Maybe you could go hunting for the Mormons!"

"They don't cancel church for people to get baptized. They have most of their baptisms on Saturday," I said. I had shared most of what I knew about the Mormons with my parents, but they rarely paid attention. To them it was another phase. I was nearly thirty years old, but to my them—especially my father—I would always be thirteen.

And behind a bush.

It took a while to figure out, but I eventually realized that I had tried to re-visit the church on the weekend of general conference. Twice a year, leaders of the LDS Church meet in Utah and give talks that are broadcast all over the world. Regular church services are not held on these weekends. Just my luck.

I didn't venture back to the church again until spring 2008. I sat alone in a pew, and a lady with curly brown hair and large round glasses approached. The size of her lenses made me think of my mother. Not because of the style but because of my mom's peculiar sense of economics.

When I first started wearing glasses myself, I opted for small lenses, and my mother saw it as a waste of money. Larger lenses meant more glass was needed, and that equaled a better value. People supersize their fries, and my mother felt it should be the same with glasses. Apparently, this lady agreed.

"It's nice to see you here. Welcome," the woman said.

"Thank you."

"Are you part of the Waterville Ward?"

"No, I'm here to visit."

"You're not a Church member?"

"No."

Before I could say anything more, she waved to someone across the room. "Get the missionaries!" she called.

"Oh, that's okay," I said. "I don't need to see them."

"I'm sure they'd love to meet you.

The new elders came like a pair of heat-seeking missiles with me as their target. Before I could blink, one of them was in my pew. His short blond hair reminded me of Elder Childs.

"It's great to meet you. I'm Elder Littlefield," he said.

We shook hands. "I've been here before. I've already done the lessons with the missionaries. You don't need to waste your time with me." It was a polite disclaimer and a warning that I wasn't as green as he thought. "Please don't feel like you have to sit with me," I told him.

I expected him to say someone else needed his attention,

but instead he shrugged. "We have to sit somewhere," he said.

I nodded, and Elder Littlefield sat, but his companion stood a second longer. The first thing I noticed about this guy was his huge smile. It was so big that I found it contagious.

"I'm Elder Nielson," he said.

He shook my hand with vigor and looked as if he were about to say something more, but the bishop had taken the pulpit and began to speak. Soon after, Elder Nielson passed me a note. It reminded me of high school when I had to hide things from the teacher. Only, in this case, it was the bishop.

"Can we have your phone number and address?" it read.

I tapped the pen he had provided against the note. I should say no, but I didn't want to be rude. I was a dead-end road for the missionaries, a polite distraction, a ditch of indecision. Of course I couldn't write that down. It was too dramatic.

But that didn't mean I couldn't do something nice for the elders. I couldn't be their investigator, but I could still be their friend even if they couldn't be mine.

"Would you like to come to dinner sometime this week?" I wrote.

When Elder Nielson saw the invitation, his eyes beamed.

And just like that, I started seeing the missionaries again. Only this time, casual visits replaced formal lessons. I fed them on occasion, and every so often they stopped by to see how I was doing or offer a spiritual thought.

Elder Nielson was such a happy-go-lucky guy that it was nearly impossible to think ill of him. Ardor radiated like a pleasant aura around him, and whether he was talking about Christ or his affinity for music and singing, his love for life was obvious. The glass was always half full. In fact, he expected it to overflow at any second.

Elder Littlefield was much more low key, but we bonded over our short statures. Neither of us could have been more than five feet seven, and even that was being generous.

"There's a saying among missionaries that when you're knocking on doors, you don't have to outrun the dog—you just have to outrun your companion," he told me. "And I'm always the one with the shortest legs."

He also noted that when I referred to Elder Luke and Childs, I called them "my elders." It was a slip of the tongue, really—the best way I could describe who they were and what they meant to me. But Elder Littlefield said it was a common occurrence among those who had grown close to missionaries in the past.

That part didn't surprise me. The relationship each investigator has with his missionaries is unique, and if the elder is sincere, not just in his faith but also in his Christian love, the friendship can be quite meaningful. The love I had for my own missionaries was sincere, and even though I had sometimes questioned their motives, I couldn't pour my own feelings down the drain.

In time, I began to call more missionaries "my elders." I wouldn't have it any other way.

May 1 rolled around, and I did not visit the church as often as I once did. In fact, it was like I had written all thoughts about conversion on a rain check, crumpled it up, and stuffed it away, perhaps never to be considered again.

I concentrated on my writing instead and went to take

pictures of the National Day of Prayer events in Augusta's capital park.

A large white pavilion had been erected in the middle of a field near the state house. It reminded me of those old religious revivals held in the South. The green dome of the state capitol building loomed in the background, and the sun shone bright enough to make me squint.

As I approached the tent, two men ran over to greet me. One of them was Elder Nielson. "I saw you walking over here, and I said, 'I know that guy! That's Dan Harrington!' " he said with his familiar grin.

"It's good to see you again," I said.

"Elder Littlefield is gone now," he informed me. "This is my new companion, Elder Smith."

Elder Smith wore a gray suit and was tall and slender with sand-colored hair. Unlike most missionaries, he had a slight maturity about his face, the kind that comes with age. I later learned that he was twenty-three. For a missionary, that's old.

"I wondered when I would run into an Elder Smith. There must be three or four of you in the mission."

"Actually, I'm the only one," he said.

"How did you guys find out about this event? You can't read the paper."

"People we're teaching told us about it," Elder Nielson said. "They told us that we should come down here."

"Well, I'm glad you're here. Let's go see what's happening."

The three of us made our way into the pavilion, where chairs were set in arced rows around a makeshift stage that consisted of nothing more than a clear space with a microphone stand. White plastic tables with pamphlets about the churches in attendance stood near the entrance.

No one could come in or out of the tent without seeing the information they displayed.

A man prayed at the microphone, and two black loudspeakers, the kind you might find in a rock concert, carried his voice through the open space. It was a good thing too. I never figured out why, but a motor was running somewhere behind the tent. It sounded like a colossal lawn mower, and the noise assaulted any semblance of peace. The people inside pretended not to hear it, but after a few moments, I got a headache. Being the professional that I am, I decided to suck it up and take my pictures for the paper.

Pastors from other churches I had written about were in attendance. A few of them even addressed the crowd. They waved to me and nodded, but not one of them came over to talk the way the missionaries had.

Every minister who took the stage prayed for a particular topic: hunger, peace, compassion. One man even prayed for the media, asking God to use it as a tool to report all the good news that was happening in the world as opposed to magnifying the bad. At that point, Elder Nielson turned to me.

"They're praying for you, Dan," he said over the clamor of the motor.

"I hope so. I need it."

Then again, maybe that's why I hadn't gotten a full-time job as a reporter yet. I was being too positive. Scandal sells, and a story about the National Day of Prayer wasn't going to make the front page.

We bowed our heads in silence for a while until I heard the elders whispering to each other.

"Do you think it would be okay for us to put stuff on the entrance table?" Elder Nielson asked me. "We have plenty of DVDs about the life of Jesus we can give away."

"Um . . ." I hesitated, trying to be diplomatic. "Most of the churches here are evangelical."

"What does that mean?" he asked.

"They might not be open to you," I said. It was the best explanation I could think of at the time.

"Who's in charge of this event?" Elder Smith asked. "Maybe we should get permission first."

I pointed to the man I knew from the Christian Civic League, a nonprofit group that helped advertise the event. The missionaries went over to talk with him, but he pointed to someone else who pointed to someone else. Finally, the elders came back to me.

"No one knows who's in charge," Elder Nielson said. "We'll put our videos out. I don't think anyone will mind."

"I hope you're right," I said.

The elders left for a few minutes and returned with a cardboard box full of DVDs and pamphlets about the life of Christ. The cover of the video was a beautiful rendering of Jesus clothed in white. As soon as they set it on display, a man no taller than I am appeared. He was balding, had a thick brown beard, and wore a scowl on his face. He stepped over to Elder Nielson.

"This is not the place or time to be converting people to your religion," he said. He didn't bother to say who he was.

"These DVDs are about the life of Jesus," Elder Nielson explained. "We just wanted to see if anyone wanted one."

"Look," the man said. "You're welcome to stay but not to look for converts." He pointed at Elder Nielson now, his finger raised in warning. The word *welcome* may have been a stretch for what he really meant.

"We didn't mean any harm," Elder Nielson said. "They're free."

"Put them back now!" the man yelled. He glared at Elder Nielson with the kind of stare men give each other before a brawl.

A group of women turned to look at the commotion, and Elder Nielson's demeanor melted into a mix of concern and embarrassment. When I saw his face change, a rush of anger blew through me.

I wanted to say something, but I couldn't think of anything that sounded even vaguely intelligent. I was ready to do more than raise my finger, at least not the index one.

That would have been a great headline too: "Reporter Pushes Man at the National Day of Prayer."

Besides, Elder Nielson was more than a foot taller than the guy. I imagined him knocking the man out. A mean right hook straight to the jaw delivered with his signature smile. But that wasn't exactly something missionaries were encouraged to do. In this case, Nielson was being the bigger man in more ways than one.

A woman from the crowd came over then and picked up one of the missionary videos. The man turned to look at her, breaking the stare he had on Elder Nielson. The woman read the back of the video, moving her lips with the words. Her small gesture alleviated the tension as we all watched her in silence. I wanted her to keep the DVD, but she shrugged and placed it back on the table as if she didn't know what all the fuss was about.

"It's all right," Elder Smith said. "It doesn't matter."

He stepped between Nielson and the nameless man to return the videos to the cardboard box from where

Elders Smith (left) and Nielson in 2008 at the LDS Church in Farmingdale. It wasn't hard to get Elder Nielson to smile. This is his usual expression.

they came. Either by coincidence or clever defiance, Elder Smith neglected to fold the lid closed. So the videos were still on display, just in an open box that he placed on the ground. Several people came over to glance down and see what the videos were, but no one took any.

The man disappeared into the crowd, but the hurt look remained on Elder Nielson's face. I placed a hand on his shoulder.

"I'm sorry that guy was mean to you."

"Oh, he wasn't that mean," he said, but his words didn't match his expression.

There was only one thing I could do to make him feel better. Luckily, I knew what it was.

"When can I take you out to eat?" I asked.

11.

OLD WORRIES

Not long after that, Elder Nielson left and in came Elder Juarez. Like most of the missionaries, he was from Utah, but he was also of Guatemalan descent. Many people assumed he was Mexican, and he found those assumptions a tad irritating.

He was shorter than most missionaries but burly, and his most prominent feature was his hair. What can I say? Some guys just have cool hair. Per mission rules it was short, but he kept it just tall enough not to break regulations. Imagine a shorter version of a dark haired James Dean style. Every so often I would catch him fixing it in the small vanity mirror of my car.

When I think of Elder Juarez, one memory stands out. I'm not sure why either because it's such a small thing, really. The first time we met, I was preparing to feed him and Elder Smith. Smith was always impartial to food. Still, I offered a list of what we could eat. Only one choice caught Elder Juarez's attention.

"Pizza!" he had said. "Pizza is always good!"

To this day, I think of Juarez as the pizza elder. I ate more of it with him than any missionary before or since. It didn't take long to learn that any reason for a meal was enough to make Elder Juarez happy. In that way, he was just like me. He would have fit in with my family perfectly.

He was also the first missionary I requested service from. Aside from teaching people about their faith, the elders performed community service. This was most frequently done each Tuesday at the Bread of Life Soup Kitchen in Augusta. There, the missionaries would prepare meals, feed the hungry, mop the floor, and do the dishes. But they could provide service for individuals as well. The most frequent request was to move furniture. The elders would move couches in and out of ward members' homes, mow lawns, rake leaves—you name it.

I never asked for anything so strenuous. I only needed one type of favor. It was something I had forgotten how to do, but as an elder, Juarez was more than proficient at it. I asked him to tie my ties.

He wanted to teach me how to do it, of course, but I had been taught before, and it never did much good. I simply didn't wear them often enough to remember. It's why I keep them tied in my closet at all times. That way, I'm always ready to throw one on, adjust it, and go. The only downside is that they eventually come loose or get mangled. That's why I needed Elder Juarez's help, and he seemed happy to oblige.

One afternoon, he was fixing some ties at my dining room table. Unlike the rest of my apartment, the dining room sported dark brown paneling, a leftover from the seventies. It might have bothered me except that the room also boasted four large windows that took up most of each wall. Because of that, it was basically a sun porch, a common feature of homes in New England.

An empty pizza box sat on the table between the elders

and me. I folded it up, tossed it in a nearby trash can, and placed two freshly pressed ties in front of Juarez. He looped one around his neck and began his work in silence. His hands wove the speckled blue and black material with barely a pause, making his chore appear far too easy.

Elder Smith looked on and sipped from a glass of water. Both elders wore short sleeves because summer had come to Maine. The brief but hot season was a treat to most Mainers and the perfect time to swim, hike, or enjoy the fleeting sun.

But for the elders, it meant long walks in the heat, and their short sleeves offered poor respite. Maybe that's why they enjoyed my company so much.

"As missionaries," I asked, "do you tell investigators about temple garments?"

"People need to visit the temple to get them, and they can't do that until they're a member for at least one full year," Elder Smith said.

"But you don't tell investigators about them?"

"Some things the ward prepares members for."

It was not a comforting thought. I had known the ward a long time, and while they were friendly enough, they were acquaintances more than anything. I knew most of them by sight or by name, but rarely both.

"Why don't you tell people about them? I mean serious, sincere investigators."

Elder Juarez tugged the knot of his last tie tight. It looked like something I would have found on a display case in the store.

"Dan, I saw you had stories about martial artists in your writing portfolio," he mentioned.

"Yes."

"When someone is learning how to use a sword, they

don't practice with real blades on the first day. They build
up to it."

"I didn't know Mormons were dangerous."

"Just don't mess with us," he said with a grin. "But
really, it's like that. People accept the gospel line upon
line, precept upon precept."

I'd later learn that this was a famous LDS phrase.

It made sense, but it also left a lot of wiggle room. Too
much, if you ask me. But then again, even in the Bible
Jesus didn't teach people everything all at once. He didn't
put the entire plan of salvation on anyone's lap. He offered
up knowledge in pieces, sort of like bite-sized portions—
the kind that were one hundred calories each.

"We have a lesson in fifteen minutes," Elder Smith
said. "We need to go."

We shook hands as we said our good-byes, but Elder
Juarez also patted me on the shoulder.

"And you let us know if anyone messes with you," he
said with a smile. "We've got your back."

* * *

On the Sundays that I visited the ward, certain members began to grow on me. Not because of personal conversations, but because of the stories they shared during
the service.

One lady named Sister Doyle struck me as especially
tenderhearted. She wasn't a nun. They don't have those
in the LDS faith. Instead, each Church member was
addressed as either "brother" or "sister" followed by their
last name. It was a way to reinforce that we're all part of
the same heavenly family.

Sister Doyle must have been in her early fifties. She
was tall and thin, with salt and pepper hair that was more

salt than pepper. She had converted to the faith from Catholicism. Given the local population, that wasn't so remarkable. Augusta had a rich Catholic tradition, but she was one of the few members to mention it.

At one sacrament meeting she shared with the ward how she had told her parents that she planned to become Mormon. Her father had three questions about the LDS Church:

Do they believe in God the Father?

Do they believe in God the Son?

Do they believe in the Holy Spirit?

When the answers were all yes, he had given her his blessing. Sister Doyle said that her parents knew the power of prayer and felt that since she believed that God had told her through prayer to join this church, it was the right thing to do.

I shared the story with my mother that day. She had just finished her breakfast. Crumbs of toast speckled the plate in front of her, and she sipped a half empty cup of juice. When I finished the story, she paused and asked her favorite question.

"Are you hungry?"

"No," I said.

"How about some pancakes? You want some pancakes?"

"Mother, what do you think of what I just told you?"

"It's crazy. The Father, the Son, and the Holy Spirit are all God. She's talking about the same thing three times," my mother said as she finished the last dribble of juice. "But if you want to join this crazy church, go ahead."

"Why do you think it's crazy?"

"They won't even let you drink. Jesus made wine and

passed it around for people. And they don't like coffee either. Coffee! What's wrong with it?"

"Those issues don't really affect me."

"If they won't let you drink coffee, what's next?" my mother asked. "Are they going to tell you when to use the bathroom too?"

"Don't be foolish! Besides, I'm not joining the Church anyway."

"You talk about it a lot."

My mother's concerns may not have been poetic, but they're important for any convert to consider. Well, except the bathroom part.

The LDS Church does ask a lot of its members. The Word of Wisdom is a sort of code that the Mormons live by. It forbids smoking and drinking coffee, tea, and alcohol. Except for the occasional happy hour, I followed the rules already.

It should have been easy to join, but the lifestyle wasn't the hard part. The problem was that the beliefs didn't match up with mine. And worse, there was that temple issue.

"So do you want some pancakes? I'm going to put everything away if you don't want them right now," my mother said.

"Well . . ." I hesitated. "I guess so."

"I knew you wanted them." And a few minutes later nothing else was on my mind except the sweet taste of maple syrup heaven.

12.

MORMON MARINE

I LIKED MEETING NEW MISSIONARIES, but I wasn't always certain they wanted to meet me. That's how I felt when I met Elder Dowling.

I greeted the missionaries outside my apartment. The sunny day matched my mood, and a late summer breeze ruffled Elder Juarez's famous hair. Elder Smith had been transferred to a new area, and once again, I did not get to say good-bye. However, I did get a call from Elder Juarez saying I should meet the new missionary right away. He sounded more excited than usual and hinted that we had something in common.

Elder Juarez was the first to exit the missionary car after they parked in front of my place. When he walked over to me, I presented him with another tie. He took it without a word, knowing what had to be done. I had bought it only a few hours earlier. It was checkered with various shades of black, and I thought it should match any color shirt in my closet. That was the genius part. Still, it was only a dapper piece of cloth until Juarez worked his magic.

That's when Elder Dowling approached. Right away, I noticed what we had in common—a shaved head. While it's certainly an excellent hairstyle, I never expected to see it on an elder.

He did not smile as we shook hands but instead gazed at me with what I interpreted as a glare. It didn't take long to guess what he was thinking. He wanted me baptized, and he wanted it now. Otherwise, I was a waste of time.

Maybe for the elders I was.

He continued looking serious when we ate. We shared a large tray of chicken and fries on a picnic table outside a neighborhood restaurant called the Red Barn. Elder Juarez wanted to eat in the sunshine, and so we did. He informed me that Elder Dowling was twenty-five years old, from Texas, and had spent time in the service.

"You were in the army?" I asked.

"The Marines," he corrected.

"Where were you stationed?"

"Iraq."

His brief answers reminded me of a Clint Eastwood movie. Elder Juarez paid little heed to the minimal conversation. He was too busy dipping his crinkled fries into a small mound of ketchup.

"Being a Marine, you've probably seen the best and worst in people," I said.

"I've seen my share of green grass, and I've seen my share of brown grass too," Dowling responded.

I wondered how much brown he would see in me.

No one talked for a while. We were too engrossed in the food or at least chewing extra long in the pretense of enjoying it.

"Elder Dowling just took some pain medication, so he's a little out of it," Juarez said, reaching for another fry. "He has some back issues."

"Back issues? What happened?"

Elder Dowling during his time in the United States Marine Corp.

"Motorcycle accident," Dowling said.

"You? You ride a motorcycle?"

He took a bite of his chicken and nodded slowly.

The conversation stumbled even worse after that. It wasn't until our second meeting that a two-way talk emerged, and when it did, it was less than comfortable.

As usual, I was feeding the elders. They were always grateful for my help, and I was happy to give it to them. I had them over to my apartment, and Elder Juarez asked about my latest project for the paper. This propelled me into a long-winded explanation of my next article. I mentioned something about God; I don't recall exactly what, but my comment prompted Elder Dowling to speak.

"Why don't you join the Church?" he asked.

"What?" I said, more taken by the change in subject than anything.

"Why don't you join The Church of Jesus Christ of Latter-day Saints?" he clarified.

I exchanged a glance with Elder Juarez, who offered

a polite smile. I had already been over this with him, but I should have known better. This was the perennial topic with missionaries.

"There are so many things I like about the Church," I explained. "But I don't share all your beliefs."

Elder Dowling stared at me, waiting. His eyes were hard as stone.

"I don't want to say anything offensive," I told him.

"I just want the truth."

At that point, I thought the missionaries would play a game of good cop and bad cop. From the look on Elder Dowling's face, it was clear which role he would take—the Clint Eastwood part.

"The temple for one," I told him. "I don't think God would hide things. You keep a lot of secrets, and I don't like that."

"You don't think God would hide things from people?" Elder Dowling said.

"No."

"Really?"

"Yes, really. No other church refuses to discuss their practices. I don't want to sign up only to find out later that I didn't believe in all the things I'd be required to do."

"Do you know that in the New Testament Jesus talks about the end of the world?"

"Of course."

"Then you know Jesus admits that He doesn't know when the end of the world is. He says that only the Father in Heaven knows."

I nodded. It was Matthew 24:36: "However, no one knows the day or the hour when these things will happen, not even the angels in heaven or the Son himself. Only the Father knows."

"God the Father didn't share something that important with the Savior Jesus Christ," Elder Dowling said. "He didn't tell Jesus, the one who died on the cross for us. The one who redeemed our sins. That's huge. Do you really think He's going to share everything with all of us?"

At that moment, I was speechless. And sometimes when I think of that conversation, I'm speechless still.

* * *

I was a kid again in catechism sitting in the front row. Not because I wanted to, but because I was late to class. All the smart kids had taken the desks out back. My friend Guy told especially funny jokes that day and had made me late. What was hilarious moments ago in the parking lot now made me want to choke him.

Sister Ruth wore a brown skirt and blouse with a small silver cross around her neck. She stood in front of the blackboard, which had the word *God* written on it in big chalky letters. She told us how everything in the universe had a beginning and an end, a start and a finish. Except God.

"He had no beginning," she said. "God always was, always is, and always will be."

A boy next to me raised his hand. He was a bit of a ruffian known for starting wrestling matches on the playground. I could see he was wrestling with this topic as well.

"How can God not have a beginning?" he asked.

"He just doesn't," Sister Ruth said. "The Bible says He's the alpha and the omega. These are old words that mean both the first and the last. It might be hard to understand. It's just something we have to take on faith."

A few kids questioned her further. One asked if she meant "the big bang," a concept he had heard about in school.

But what was strange to the others, I accepted. I didn't need a big explanation to believe God had no beginning. Just like I didn't need a hundred reasons to believe in Jesus. I just knew what Sister Ruth had said was true.

Some things need no explanation. At least not to me.

13.

A DONUT TO REMEMBER

THE NEXT SUNDAY AFTER CHURCH, Elder Juarez asked for a ride back to the missionary apartment. I was surprised no ward member was assigned such a duty, but their apartment was on my way home anyway.

We went down the hall to where Elder Dowling had been talking with a group of ward members and found him bent down on one knee. A little girl, who looked no more than ten years old, was staring at him. She flashed a brief grin but held close to her mother's skirt.

"Watch this," Elder Dowling told her.

He lifted the end of his tie out in front of his face like a small pyramid that faced up toward the ceiling. Then, he let out a long, exaggerated breath as if he were blowing out the candles of a birthday cake. As he did so, the tip of his tie fell like a wilted flower. A second later, it shot back up to its original shape.

"Do you want to try it?" he asked.

The little girl bit her lip and shook her head. Behind her smile, she looked a little scared of Elder Dowling, and I didn't blame her. I was a little scared of him myself.

But here, with the little girl, his stern eyes were nowhere to be found. Instead, he boasted a playful grin.

"I'll try again and see if it works," he said.

Once again he blew, and the end of his tie magically drooped. The little girl had a skeptical look in her eye, but she inched closer to him until the tie popped back up. Her hesitation went on for quite some time until the adults nearby also urged her to try it.

I probably would have given up, but Elder Dowling patiently waited as the child grew more accustomed to him.

Finally, she blew toward the tie, and the pyramid tip crumbled the way it had so many times before. The effect amused the girl, and she laughed and hopped in place, clutching her mother's hand.

When Dowling stood back on both feet, Elder Juarez informed him that I would be bringing them back to their apartment.

"So can I try that trick too?" I joked.

Dowling just stared at me with no reply. Clint Eastwood was at it again.

* * *

Not long after that, Elder Juarez left and in came Elder Kelsey. He was a tall young man with red hair and large brown eyes that gleamed with youth and excitement. I took him and Elder Dowling to Red Robin so we could get better acquainted and insisted they order anything they wanted.

"Wow!" Elder Kelsey exclaimed. "I hope I stay in Augusta for six months!"

"He's not going to treat us like this every week," Elder Dowling scolded, but I'm not sure his companion heard. Elder Kelsey was too busy reading the menu the way a young boy might read a treasure map. A hint of Elder Childs was in him.

At that point, something startled me. An object flew passed my ear. It went so fast that I couldn't tell what it was. I only knew that it went directly at Elder Dowling.

The waitress had seen what happened and darted over to our table.

"I'm so sorry," she said.

My first thought was that someone shot a spitball at us, and if so, Elder Dowling was the wrong missionary to mess with. He looked down in his lap and pulled up a thin crumbled shard of paper, the kind that covers straws. It was dry.

"A little girl did it by mistake," the waitress explained. "She blew into her straw and the end of the paper shot out."

Elder Dowling grinned. "Don't worry about it. It was funny." He waved at the parents behind me who echoed the waitress's apology.

"I'm glad to see you have a sense of humor," I told him.

"Actually I left it in the car," he said.

"I thought you left it in Texas."

"That's right," he said. "I left it in the car in Texas."

We both grinned.

"So what kind of things does a Marine do for fun when he's not on his mission?"

"Ride bikes."

"Dirt bikes?"

"Motorcycles," he said.

"Harleys?"

"Sport bikes. I started a bike club with some guys I know."

"So . . ." I paused. "You were in a gang?

"That's what I said too!" Elder Kelsey interjected.

*Elder Dowling performs a stunt on his bike prior
to his mission.*

"Man, it wasn't a gang," Dowling complained. "I used to get a lot of comments about that. We raised money for charities and did volunteer work."

"Was that between your gang fights?" I asked.

"It wasn't a gang!"

"So did you guys have a name?" I asked.

"Endangered Species," he said.

"And you should see his bike too," Elder Kelsey said. "He had a sweet silver one. It was like something out of James Bond."

"Had?" I said. "Why had?"

"I sold it to go on my mission," Elder Dowling said.

"That's right. You guys have to pay ten grand to go on your missions. It must have been hard to sell."

"The Lord is worth it," Dowling told me.

It was then that I realized how prejudiced I had been. Elder Dowling didn't look like the other missionaries, nor did he smile much, but that didn't mean he was angry with me.

Maybe that's one thing I liked about the elders. They were always polite and friendly. Over time, I came to expect to see certain traits in them. But Elder Dowling was much closer to my age, and his experience in the Marines had tarnished my crystal ball. I didn't know what to think, so I expected something negative. That said more about me than it did about him.

"You had mentioned that you were a convert to the Church," I said.

"I was a Baptist," he told me.

"What made you change?"

"Some missionaries met with me, and when I prayed about the Book of Mormon, I knew it was true."

"You make it sound so simple."

"I follow where the Lord leads. I became a missionary to help others do the same," he said.

For the rest of the meal, we joked and laughed and talked about God. Elder Dowling wasn't like the other elders, but he was still a good guy. Strange how a gang member made me realize that.

* * *

A few days later, something special entered the picture: a donut. It wasn't a pastry or confection. In fact, you couldn't eat it at all. But it was memorable nonetheless.

I had planned to rendezvous with the missionaries at their apartment, but I spotted them riding their bikes on the way. Elder Dowling was in the lead on State Street while Kelsey lagged behind.

I pulled into the parking lot to their apartment. It was a long rectangle nestled between their home and an office building. Cars were crammed together, and I had to park behind a large black van. The building they lived in was three stories high with a large porch that overlooked the busy street. The missionaries lived on the first floor, and a picture of Jesus hung in the window.

Elder Dowling pulled in front of my car but kept his eyes on the road for his companion. I barely had time to step out and greet him when it happened.

At the far side of the parking lot, Elder Kelsey yelled something I couldn't decipher. He dove down into a sharp dip in the pavement and then went up in the air. It looked like something Evil Kenevil might do but had a less than satisfying result.

While airborne, the bike wavered. Elder Kelsey's arms flailed. Right away, I knew something was wrong. A car blocked my vision as he fell, but the sound of the crash was unmistakable.

"Excuse me," Elder Dowling said as he left to check on his companion.

I hesitated, not knowing if I should go look too. Kelsey was probably embarrassed. I would have been.

By the time I came around the cars, the elders were walking their bikes toward me. Elder Kelsey winced in pain, and Dowling shook his head with a silly grin.

"Here, let me take your bike so you don't have to carry it," I told Elder Kelsey. He let go of it gladly. The back wheel was tangled into a warped crescent of spokes and tire. It wasn't pretty.

"Are you all right?" I asked.

"I don't know," he said.

"What happened? Couldn't you avoid that dip in the pavement?"

"I was trying a bike trick Elder Dowling showed me. It didn't work out too well."

"I noticed."

The missionaries went inside to check on Elder Kelsey, and I rested the bikes against the porch railing. They returned about five minutes later.

"What's wrong?" I asked. "Where are you hurt?"

"In the back," Elder Kelsey said.

"Yeah, the *lower* back," Dowling added.

Kelsey motioned to his behind, and his companion chuckled.

"What does it look like? Is it bleeding?"

"It's not bleeding, but I can't see it," Kelsey explained. "There's only one mirror in our apartment."

"Maybe someone should take a look at it," I suggested, looking at Elder Dowling.

"I'm not doing it," he said. "We're friends, but we're not that close."

"But he's hurt."

"Dan, you've always said that if there's anything you could do to help us, you'd do it."

"There are some things only a mission companion can do," I insisted.

Kelsey tried to shake off the pain, but a few hours later he wound up in the hospital. The diagnosis—a fractured tail bone.

They gave him some painkillers and recommended a donut. That's right, an inflatable ring to sit on. The first one reminded me of one of those floaty things children use at the beach. By sitting on it, Elder Kelsey could relieve the pressure on his buttocks and, voilà, less pain.

Unfortunately, the first one didn't work out too well. It popped during church. Either the hard pew or Elder Kelsy's rear end had been too much for the poor thing. He needed something less precarious. The second donut was a

Elder Kelsey poses with his donut. The cushion helped relieve his pain after his bicycle accident.

cushion. It couldn't pop, but its tan color reminded me of a real-life honey-dipped confection.

"They should have put some chocolate glaze on this one," I joked. "It would have been more appealing."

"I wanted sprinkles on it," Kelsey said.

We took several pictures of Elder Kelsey with the donut, and to this day, I can't think of him without it. Superman had his S, Wonder Woman had her lasso, and Elder Kelsey had his donut.

14.

SHADES OF BELIEF

WRITING FOR THE PAPER OFFERED the chance to dabble in all sorts of interests. One Saturday I interviewed professional wrestlers, and the next day I attended a Jehovah's Witnesses' convention. My editor got a big laugh out of that. What can I say? I'm versatile.

I visited a lot of churches during that time. I liked the LDS Church, but there was definitely room for improvement. Perhaps another place of worship could offer it.

I went to an ecumenical talent show where several denominations were raising money for a local food bank called the Chrysalis Place. It was an odd name indeed. Maybe they thought being poor was like being in a cocoon, and financial independence was like becoming a butterfly. Who knows?

A pastor from a local Baptist church opened the evening with a prayer and said that anyone who had questions about finding a relationship with the Lord was welcome to speak to him after the show.

Five minutes after the final curtain, the same pastor started shutting the lights off, asking everyone to leave so he could lock the church door. If anyone had any questions about faith, they were encouraged to ask immediately after the applause. No dilly-dallying allowed. In his defense, I'm sure there was a suggestion box where deep, philosophical questions could have been dropped off.

Before the lights went dark, I managed to sneak in a far too brief interview with one of the performers. After my third or fourth question, the pastor repeated—in my general direction—that the lights were being turned off. It sounded like the church building was more important than the people. At least the Mormons never kicked me out.

Another time, I had the distinct displeasure of attending an obnoxious Bible study group. It took place in the back room of a small antique shop in the heart of the city. About a dozen people gathered in a circle as a girl who might have been twenty years old conducted the lesson. She had stringy blonde hair and wore a white tube top that looked more appropriate for a dance club than a church group.

I sat on a hard plastic chair next to a lady who looked familiar. She thought I did too, but neither of us could place where we had seen the other. She had jet black hair that flirted with her shoulders and wore a purple blouse with white stripes across the waist.

Two people whispered something to each other when the lesson began, and the girl in the tube top went ballistic.

"Shut up!" she scolded. "Everyone shut up! It's time to read from the Holy Bible!" She placed a special emphasis on the word *holy*.

I had never been told to "shut up" and be holy at the same time, but I must have been the only one. Everyone else was oblivious to the lack of reverence and opened their Bibles to the appropriate passage. We read from Habakkuk: "I will be joyful in the God of my salvation. The Sovereign Lord is my strength. He will give me the speed of a deer and bring me safely over the mountains" (Habakkuk 3:18–19).

"Wow, what a beautiful passage," the shut-up girl said. "God can make us fast as deer."

"That's pretty fast when you think about it," someone agreed.

A young man about the age of my elders raised his hand. He had curly black hair and awful teenage acne, the kind I was thankful to lose. The shut-up girl called on him. "That's just this translation," he said. "The deer, I mean. He can make us fast like other things too. Even faster, I bet."

Suggestions came in a flurry.

"An elk."

"A horse is pretty fast."

"How about a stallion?"

"A bullet."

"Yeah, but you have to think about the context," the boy said. "They didn't have bullets in those days."

"No," someone else agreed. "But they had arrows, and arrows are pretty fast."

The conversation soon changed from bullets and arrows to miraculous healings. Everyone knew I was from the paper, so they started sharing second- and third-hand accounts of incredible events. I don't recall the specifics of each story because the tales tumbled over each other, one at a time, as if each member of the circle couldn't wait for his or her chance to speak. I'm pretty sure God helped one lady with a gastro-intestinal problem.

At that point the woman beside me gasped.

"Oh, I remember where we met, Dan," she said. "You hit me at the rotary one morning! We were in an accident."

Her words jolted my memory into place. The year prior on my way to work, she had braked suddenly when I was behind her on the rotary entrance. My car tapped hers. And when I say tapped, I mean it. The impact was so slight that I wasn't sure if we had collided at all. But she had gotten out of her car to inspect for damage, so I had known something was wrong.

We had pulled to the side of the road where neither of us could find a scratch. She had dismissed it at the time, but two days later I got a call from my insurance company that a woman was claiming more than $500 worth of damage to her vehicle. I was so angry at the time.

All this must have shown on my face as we sat in the Bible study. I tried to cover it up, but I've never been very good at that. Where was Elder Luke when I needed him?

"Oh, don't worry about it," she said to me. "I forgive you. I'm a Christian."

That night when I left, I knew the article about the Bible study group would be rejected from the get-go. Not only that, but I was disgusted at how these people were in the dark about respect and reverence. If these were the choices I had, the Mormons were in the lead. No question about it.

* * *

Elder Dowling passed the sacrament bread to me at church the next Sunday. I took hold of the silvery tray he held and ate a piece of bread before passing it on to the next person in the pew.

The act itself was symbolic of what Elder Dowling was

trying to do. He had a particular faith and was sharing it with me in the hope that I would accept it, take it, and later own it for myself.

My sister once said that medieval priests were every bit as brave as soldiers when they went into foreign lands to spread the faith. We don't know the names of these men, but their overall effect was present everywhere. Without them, Christianity would never have become the world religion it was today. And without men like Elder Dowling, the LDS Church wouldn't have grown the way it has either.

I remembered when I took what the Catholic Church calls the First Communion. Sister Ruth was at it again, stressing reverence during the ritual. To highlight how important it was, we had a special dress rehearsal in church. She demonstrated how we should cup our hands, one over the other, as we approached the altar.

"Now, when you get up to the priest, he's going to hold up the Eucharist and say, 'The body of Christ.' You reply by saying, 'Amen,' " Sister Ruth said.

First the hand cupping and then an "amen." To my young mind, it felt like a lot to remember, and I hoped I wouldn't mess it up.

If we didn't want to cup our hands, we had the option of leaving our mouths open. The priest could also set the bread on our tongue. It was an interesting variation that I rejected right away. It just didn't seem right to have anyone's hands that close to my mouth, especially in church.

Besides, what if I got nervous and said "amen" when I shouldn't? The wafer might fall to the floor. Then I'd be in real trouble with the Lord. All sorts of things could go wrong, and I had to get it right. I had to.

The funny thing is that I remember the rehearsal more than taking the actual communion. It must have been a success. I cupped my hands correctly. I said a good amen, and soon it was just another part of going to church.

Temple garments were probably like that too. A lot of worry, an anticlimax, and then the subtle swing into normalcy.

I had already been exposed to more LDS culture than I ever expected. Things that seemed so strange at first had acclimated into my life quite well. Habits like going to church for three hours, talking with the missionaries, and reading the Book of Mormon weren't as bad as I once believed.

But the experience also reminded me of a fable someone once shared at the LDS Church. It was about a nomad in the desert who pitched his tent during a terrible sandstorm. A wild camel had come his way and asked if it could keep its head inside the tent, near the ceiling, an area of the shelter the nomad wasn't using. This would keep sand out of the camel's tender eyes and not bother the nomad at all, the camel argued.

Being charitable, the nomad agreed to this, but over time, the camel claimed more and more space until the nomad was kicked out of his own tent. The story was used to illustrate how sin works and how small acts can take over a person's life.

But it also made me think of my own faith. Becoming Mormon didn't just mean accepting new beliefs; it meant tossing out the old. The hardest to give away were the traditional beliefs about God—beliefs that most Christians, not just Catholics, profess.

The missionaries didn't believe that Jesus was God incarnate, but rather that he was God's Son, an entirely separate being who was still our Savior and part of what the Latter-day Saints called the Godhead rather than the Trinity. They also believed in a Heavenly Mother, a figure seldom discussed but believed to be present. And, of course, there was the temple. To me, it was like a colossal stop sign telling me not to proceed. These ideas were hard to swallow. In fact, they had gotten caught in my spiritual throat like jagged bones ready to choke me. They grated against everything I knew to be true. I couldn't help but wonder how other investigators dealt with these issues or if they even bothered to question the elders about them at all.

15.

"DEATH" OF AN ELDER

"IS IT THE GODHEAD?" ELDER Dowling said. "Is that what bothers you so much?"

I was giving the elders a ride home again when Elder Dowling asked the question. I had just pulled into the parking lot to their place. It felt like we had a long conversation ahead of us, so I pulled the key from the ignition. He sat beside me in the car while Elder Kelsey was in the backseat with his donut.

"That's problematic, but I understand how you can think that way," I said.

"Then what is it, Dan? What's still stopping you?"

"I've told you—the temple. The ideas about the nature of God. I just don't know what to think about it all."

"You're looking too far ahead. It's like you're on the third step of a ladder, and you're obsessed with step seventeen. You have to take one step at a time. That's what precept upon precept means."

"Put one foot in front of the other until you fall into the font, huh?" I said.

"Dan, you can do it. You're just looking beyond the mark," Kelsey said.

"Becoming a member means giving up beliefs that

have always been important to me. If I have this many questions now, what will it be like when missionaries stop coming?"

"Then you pray about it," Kelsey said.

"If this was the right choice, don't you think it would be easier? What if I encounter something I know is wrong after baptism? I'm already seeing a lot of red flags here."

"You can always leave," Elder Dowling said. "I would leave if the Church taught something I knew wasn't true."

"You would?" His answer startled me.

"Yes, but the Church is true. I know it because God let me know through prayer. He's not going to give me a different answer than He gives you."

It was the best argument Elder Dowling could have made. We could have gone over the Book of Mormon point by point. We could have read every anti-Mormon pamphlet ever created. But none of it would have been as convincing as Elder Dowling's testimony.

Let's face it. He lived his faith far better than I lived mine. He had been to war, and done things I would never want to do. He didn't flaunt his faith in Jesus the way some so-called Christians did. He just lived it and shared what he knew with others.

It was one thing to second-guess the Church, but I could never question Elder Dowling's faith in Christ. Not ever.

"Isn't a transfer coming up for you two?" I asked. It was probably best to change the subject.

"Pretty soon," Elder Kelsey said.

"Are you wondering where you might be headed?"

"I don't have to," Dowling told me. "I'm going home. My two years are almost up."

"They are?"

"Yep, I'm going to die. When elders start the mission, we joke that they're born. When they go home, we say they die."

"I get to kill him," Kelsey added.

"I read that you guys usually do a good-bye ceremony, like cutting a tie or burning a shirt."

Dowling tossed the end of his tie over his shoulder like a scarf. "No one's cutting one of my ties!"

"He's very protective of his ties," Elder Kelsey said.

"I'll probably burn a shirt, though. I've got a few that could use it," Dowling said. "We should get going, but we'll catch up with you soon."

I watched the elders walk up the steps into their apartment and wondered if I was being too hard on their church. I had read so much about it that at times, it drove me crazy. Catholic, Protestant, and LDS doctrine all collided in a huge traffic jam inside my head. And all of them were honking their horns.

Elder Kelsey once admitted that he wished he knew more about other faiths the way I did. I told him that not knowing kept the road clear. Only small patches of mud were on his path to heaven. I had big messy clumps on mine.

But the Catholic Church had always been a beacon to me, a call to the shore of my faith. It was the ruler by which I measured truth. I sometimes got sidetracked by other faiths, mostly in an academic sense. But the Latter-day Saints were like the sirens of Greek myth, calling out for me to join their island. And I could feel the pull.

Only my problems with their deep doctrine kept me anchored. I had found out about the temple garments on my own, and when I did, it felt like the elders were trying

Elder Dowling prepares to shovel the mission vehicle during his first New England winter. He was in Vermont at the time.

to fool me into the Church. My reaction was to study every LDS practice and dogma I could.

But was that entirely fair? Most churches had a few strange ideas hidden somewhere in their attics, things that were also hard to accept. The Catholic Church taught transubstantiation, the idea that the communion bread spiritually became the body of Christ, not just a symbol of it. Some Protestants celebrated eternal security, the idea that if you accept Jesus as the Savior, you can rob, rape, and murder and still have perfect assurance of getting to heaven.

Yet I kept the Mormons under a microscope because their attic felt bigger than most churches. It was as if I had gone to a monastery and demanded to know all the rules, from top to bottom, before I would sign up. It didn't do much good either, because I would never have all the facts.

I'd never see all their practices unless I joined. At first, something about that struck me as sinister. But the more time I spent at church and the more I prayed, even that feeling had started to subside. Oh, it was still there. It had just morphed into a background noise instead a blaring alarm.

Why was I thinking about baptism so much anyway? I had already decided not to do it. It was all Elder Dowling's fault. Never trust a Mormon marine.

* * *

I don't remember saying good-bye to Elder Dowling mostly because we never really needed to say it. He's been to see me twice since he finished his mission and calls me more often than any other elder.

I asked him once if he was ever angry with the Lord. While in Augusta, he had gone to the chiropractor several times with back pain. A doctor at the Veteran's hospital at Togus recommended surgery for the pinched discs in his spine.

Elder Dowling said he contemplated that choice, but he knew that a corrective surgery could cause more damage. Weeks in the hospital didn't appeal to him nor did the possibility of being paralyzed. So instead, he postponed surgery indefinitely to see how long he could live with the chronic pain.

He had served his country during the unpopular war in Iraq and God for two years as a missionary. Why couldn't he just be healed?

When I mentioned it to him, he looked puzzled. "Why would I be angry with God? What good would that do? Besides, He must want me to learn something from this," he said.

Little things like that made me respect his faith even more. In fact, I felt a bit inadequate as a Christian. Faith in Jesus wasn't about who read the Bible the most, who could quote the most scripture, or who made the best argument. It wasn't even about who goes to what church. It's in the way we live our lives. I admired Elder Dowling for the way he lived his.

He always said that the mission had changed his life forever. Soon it would do so again. A female missionary called him to schedule a reunion for returned missionaries from New England. From what I understand, one thing led to another, and the two were married in 2009. He and his wife bought a house in Texas, and Elder Dowling told me that being married was better than he ever imagined.

In a 2010 phone conversation, I asked if he had been hanging out with his old biker gang.

"Not really. It's not a good idea to ride with my back the way it is," he said. "Plus, I don't have a bike anymore since I sold it."

"Can't you ride on the back of someone else's bike?" I asked with feigned sincerity. I had learned from television that bikers had an unkind name for the back seat.

Elder Dowling must have known the seat's reputation. There was a long pause on the other end of the phone. His tone grew serious.

"That's not how I roll," he said.

16.

A TALE OF TWO TITANS

NORMALLY WHEN ONE MISSIONARY leaves, the other stays behind, so naturally I assumed that would happen with Elder Kelsey. I was wrong.

He called me up the day before transfers to say he was leaving too. He was just as surprised as I was, but he wished me well and said he would keep me in his prayers. I took it as a sign that my time with elders was at an end. For the second time, I was wrong.

I found out from my neighbor that the new missionaries had knocked on my door when I wasn't home, so I decided to give them a call.

"Hello, this is Elder Pry-ba-la-ba," a voice answered.

I had no idea what he said. I caught a P and that was it. Whatever his name was, it was a mouthful. I introduced myself as a friend of the elders, and he recognized my name.

"Hi, Dan! I'm brand new!" he said. His excitement reminded me of Elder Nielson. It was a good sign.

We set up a time to meet so that I could show him and his companion the Augusta area. I knocked on their apartment door at the appointed time, and as soon as it opened, I was in the presence of giants.

Although their faces betrayed their youth, these elders were built like titans. One was blond, and the other had red hair. Their sturdy builds and light complexion reminded me of Viking warriors. These guys could have easily donned a pair of horned helmets.

I reached out to shake the blond one's hand. He was the shorter of the two, but he was still tall enough to tower over me. His name was Elder Bailey.

His companion was the guy I spoke with on the phone, but even seeing his name tag didn't help.

"How do you pronounce your name again, Elder?"

"Prybylinski," he said.

"Purple what?"

"Prybylinksi."

"Pry-bye . . . . Can you say it one more time?"

"You can call me Elder P," he said.

"It's a deal!"

As we packed into my car, I never realized how small a Ford Escort was. We stopped for a meal and asked the typical questions people ask when they first meet. Elder Bailey was the senior companion. He was from Alaska but had grown up as a military brat, moving here and there across the country. The Church had served as a constant for him. Wherever he went, it was a place to feel at home and make friends.

Elder P, meanwhile, was from Idaho and had grown up on a farm.

"Sometimes I hated milking goats in the morning before school," he said.

"You milked goats?" I asked. "I didn't know people did that anymore."

"Where do you think milk comes from?"

"Cows," I said.

Elder Bailey takes a break at a stream just outside of Augusta. The bridge is part of a park in Hallowell called "Hobbit Land."

"People drink goat's milk too," he told me.

I guess they did, but I didn't realize it happened in the United States. I thought it was in places like Zimbabwe, Malaysia, and other countries I needed a globe to find.

Had I met Elder P the year prior, his answer would have been something I might expect from a Mormon. Now I realized how unusual it was.

I gave them a brief tour of Augusta's hot spots, which for the elders meant finding Walmart, the local hospital, and the nearest grocery store.

"Do you guys want to get a quick ice cream at McDonald's before I take you home?" I asked.

"Sure," Elder Bailey said.

"Dan, you're spoiling us!" Elder P added.

"That's my job," I told him.

When we got to McDonald's, I ordered three sundaes, but when I turned from the counter to hand the missionaries theirs, a man stepped between us. He was my height with stringy brown hair that went every which way on his balding head. A plaid flannel shirt stuck out from his belt in haphazard fashion, and his baggy pants were unkempt and wrinkled.

"So that's what you are?" he was saying. "Missionaries? From what church?

Elder P answered, and the man rolled his eyes. "Not that hogwash! You'd be surprised how much I know. I know a lot about church!"

Terrific, I thought. *Just the thing to spoil a good ice cream.*

"Thank you, sir. Have a good day," I said.

I gave the elders their sundaes, and with my head, I motioned the elders to follow me deeper into the restaurant where I claimed a booth. They followed me, but so did the man. Talk about an unwelcome surprise.

As we sat, he stood at the edge of our booth with wild eyes that shifted back and forth between us. It was as if he was trying to warn us of imminent danger, and we were being far too casual about it.

It might have been a little worrisome if I hadn't been with a couple of titans. Elder P looked at the man with concern in his eyes, but Elder Bailey had an air of experience about him. He had dealt with this type of situation before, and I had the impression that he wasn't afraid of getting physical.

Later on, I dubbed Elder Bailey the Alaskan Mauler. It would be his ring name if he ever became a pro-wrestler or cage fighter. He thought it was funny and adopted it as a personal nickname.

"Sir, we're trying to eat," I said to the crazy man.

He looked me up and down. "You're not one of them, are you?"

"No."

It didn't take Batman to figure out I wasn't a missionary. Not only was I sans name tag, but my blue jeans and red sweater were a dead giveaway.

He leaned closer to the elders and pointed at me with his thumb. "This guy is a bad influence on you, and I know these things."

"So do you go to church?" Elder P asked.

"I don't have time for that crap," the man said. "I know where to get real answers."

"Prayer, you mean?" Elder P said.

"No! I have something much better."

The man reached into his pant pocket and fished out a slender chain. A small, polished stone hung at the end. He held it up for us to see. "The pendulum," he proclaimed as if we were in a scene from *Lord of the Rings*. "This gives us real answers."

The elders and I stared at it in silence. Was he even serious? Were we on *Candid Camera*?

"Ask it a question."

"Sir, we're busy right now," I said.

"Ask it!" he insisted. "Ask it!"

"Is the Bible true?"

He dangled the chain from his thumb and index finger. It swung back and forth. "Yes and no. That means some of it's true," he explained.

"Is the Pearl of Great Price true?"

"What's that?" he said to me.

"Ask the pendulum," I said.

It was fun throwing his words back at him. The book was a lesser-known LDS scripture, and I was curious if the man had heard of it. He hadn't, and for that matter, the pendulum didn't know it either. It swung counter clockwise. I'm sorry to report that this meant the scripture was phony. Latter-day Saints everywhere must be shaking in their boots.

"When you move your hand a certain way, you decide which direction the pendulum swings," Elder P said.

"No, I don't!" the man yelled as if the idea was ludicrous.

The conversation sunk deeper into a mire of obsurdity. The pendulum provided a way to communicate with higher realms. Gods and spirits moved the chain, not his hand. To think otherwise was foolish.

"And you can make your pendulum out of anything you want. Any combination of rope or twine with any weight you can imagine," he was saying.

"We have to get going now," I said, standing. Our sundaes were gone, and I gathered the plastic cups from the elders to throw in the trash.

Elder P tried to give the man a pass-along card and said he'd like to tell him about The Church of Jesus Christ of Latter-day Saints, but the man swatted the card away and said the elders had nothing to teach him.

We left the restaurant and filed back into my car.

"That was sad but funny. We'll remember that for a long time," I said.

"I might make a pendulum out of a rolled up tube sock," Elder Bailey joked.

All three of us busted out in laughter. A nice way to relieve the tension. Such events are far better as memories than when they actually happen.

It was December 2008. Christmas time. The season when more people are apt to think of the Savior—except maybe me, the missionaries, and Sister Ruth. I suspect that we think about him more often than most.

Snow returned with the bitter frost, the kind I had to scrape off my car. The elders bought enormous puffy black coats with heavy hoods that were akin to something Eskimos might wear. Elder Bailey joked that he could use his as a tent if he ever needed to make an emergency shelter.

I invited the missionaries to Mass one Saturday evening, and they accepted. Elder Bailey had been to a Catholic Mass once, but Elder P hadn't. They were both curious about what it would be like to attend a church service in New England.

We went to St. Augustine's, one of the three Catholic churches in Augusta. Built at the peak of an area known as Sand Hill, it overlooked Augusta's downtown district as well as the banks of the Kennebec River. A gold colored statue of Christ greeted us as we approached the church. Like St. Mary's on the other side of city, St. Augustine's boasted tripled-arched doors. Above the center doorway, a single looming spire topped with a slender cross rose up into the purple evening sky.

The inside of the church could hold around two hundred people, so when I opened the door, I was shocked to find every pew full. People were shoulder to shoulder. You could have found more room in a pack of gum.

Scanning through the pews, I finally spotted a few empty spaces, but only here and there. Nothing looked big enough to hold two Viking warriors plus me.

"I don't think we'll be able to sit together," I said.

"Oh no, we're sitting with you," Elder Bailey told me.

He pointed to a small pew on the left hand side of the church. It was near the back row and had only one man sitting in it. *Hallelujah*! I thanked God and went straight for it.

A few people I knew saw me then. They waved but remained in their seats. When I reached the pew, I asked the man if it was okay to sit with him.

"Certainly," he said. He stood up and let us pass so he could remain sitting closest to the aisle.

The pew could only handle the four of us. If anyone sneezed, the man at the end might have been bumped to the floor. The priest had already started talking from the pulpit, but I couldn't see his face. A pillar that we later dubbed "the holy pillar" blocked him from view.

Even still, St. Augustine's was a far cry from what the elders were used to, and I watched as they studied their surroundings. Two rows of white pillars stretched toward a vaulted ceiling overhead, and mosaics of multi-colored glass surrounded us like an army of luminous sentinels. Each one boasted an ornate stained glass centerpiece that depicted a holy object from angels to the Holy Spirit in the form of a dove. Other than the windows, everything else was a pristine white. It reminded me of heaven, and I wondered if any of it reminded the elders of the temple.

At the front of the room, a large crucifix was fixed to the wall. It bore a statue of Jesus wearing the crown of thorns. Elder P looked at it with pursed lips as if he didn't know what to make of such a thing. I would have whispered to ask what he was thinking, but this was a time to be quiet, or so I thought.

A heater on the wall beside me rattled and popped. Soon hot air hissed out of the vent. Like a snake's warm breath, it poured out in a long "sssss" sound. No wonder the pew had been free.

I couldn't help but feel a touch of embarrassment. It felt like the elders had shown up at my house on a bad laundry day when my clothes were strewn about the sofa.

They were supposed to see the beauty of the church, not be distracted by the hiss of a heater.

Elder Bailey leaned close to my ear. "They're not trying to gas us, are they?"

We both chuckled in our seats, but his words helped put me at ease.

For the rest of the hour, we went through the usual motions: standing, sitting, kneeling. By pressing my shoulder against the heater, I was able to create a good half-inch between Elder Bailey and myself. It offered enough room for us to get up and down without bumping each other too much.

We recited the "Our Father" prayer, something I was surprised the missionaries were able to do. It was one of my favorite parts of Mass. Hearing a whole church repeat words that Jesus once spoke was a unique experience and one that I always enjoyed. Plus, I knew what to expect. At certain points in the service, I floundered and copied whatever my neighbors were doing, but when it came to the Lord's Prayer, I knew every word.

Eventually we came to the infamous "peace be with you" segment, when people acknowledge each other and wish fellow congregates peace. As a child, I was awkward and shy and hated that part. As an adult, I may not have been any less awkward, but it didn't bother me nearly as much.

I shook hands with Elder Bailey first to demonstrate how it was done. Elder P watched, and the two were fast learners. Members of the congregation greeted them with bright smiles then. No one seemed to notice the Mormon name tags, and it was good to see the elders treated with kindness. Other churches may not have offered such a warm reception.

*Elders P and Bailey attended a service with
me at St. Augustine's.*

The priest gave his homily, and I prayed under my
breath. When would I have my answer? Not something I
could explain away or interpret ten different ways. Something solid. Something definite. Something I could hold
on to with both hands.

Although I could not see the priest, his voice filled
the church, loud and clear, a sound that lifted my heart to
heaven. For so long, that's what I thought of the Catholic
Church. It was my tether to God, a witness to Christ, and
a face to my faith.

Nuns like Sister Ruth or the priest who now spoke
never came into my life like the elders, but they had been
on the periphery of my vision for many more years. These
clergy reminded me that Jesus still affected people's lives.

In their own way, the elders did the same. Was one more right than the other?

"Have you ever noticed that when we talk about God, we use a lot of metaphors?" the priest asked. "He is our shepherd, our king, and our Savior. But none of these descriptions can fully encompass what God is. Perhaps his works are mysterious because He is mysterious. The human mind cannot fully comprehend the glory that is God our Eternal Father. Anyone who claims to know too much about him isn't dealing with God, but rather, with something else."

My muscles tensed, and I took a deep breath, making sure to look straight ahead. The elders believed God was more like us than I ever imagined. The Bible said we were made in his image. According to the elders, this meant he had a body like us, and because we're his children, we could grow to be like him.

It was a persuasive argument, but what the priest said was compelling too. In fact, the priest's words were more powerful because they were born of humility, a place I believed God to be. No matter how well the elders explained it, the doctrine of exaltation made me uncomfortable, even more uncomfortable than a hissing heater.

When we left the church, I asked the elders what they thought about the service.

"Last time I went, maybe thirteen people were in the whole place. It was actually quieter than I expected for so many people," Elder Bailey said.

"It was interesting," Elder P added.

When I dropped the elders off at their apartment, I promised to see them at their church the next day. And as I drove away, the question they asked—the same question all elders asked—came to mind. Was the Book of Mormon true?

It was a complex question. The book taught that Jesus was the Savior. No matter what else it said—what else the church believed—the Book of Mormon contained what was to me the most important truth of all.

17.

CHRISTMAS & BEYOND

"SO HAVE YOU THOUGHT ABOUT getting baptized?" Elder Bailey asked.

The elders had been knocking on doors all afternoon and decided to take a short respite from the snow at my house. I had just hung his Eskimo coat beside Elder P's in the back room when Elder Bailey plopped himself in my blue recliner. He loved that chair and always called dibs on it when he arrived.

"Yes, actually, I have," I said.

"And?"

"What do you think?"

"Oh, man!" Elder Bailey said. "One of these days it will be a 'yes.' "

"I'm surprised you still talk to me with the number of times I've turned you down."

"Maybe if we were talking about football, we'd stop coming, but we always talk about the gospel. Dan, you're one of the few people around here who likes to discuss scripture without being contentious."

"Some people do use Bible quotes like weapons," I agreed.

"Well, for the record, I think you'll get baptized

someday when you're ready. It might be in twenty years. Elder P's son will come here as a missionary and say his dad told him all about you."

"And he'll know how cool you are, Dan," Elder P said. He had taken his place on the sofa and listened with a smile. I retrieved an extra chair for myself from the dining room.

"So why do you guys think I haven't converted? Most people seem to get caught up in little things like coffee or smoking, not doctrine," I said.

"Satan knew that wouldn't work with you," Elder Bailey said. "So instead he threw all this information at you that you weren't ready to handle. It reminds me of something we heard at a mission conference.

"A storm had blown this huge tree down. So, our mission president asked how the wind could knock over something so big. The answer was that the roots hadn't grown deep enough. When you pray, you have all these issues swirling around you like that storm, and your roots haven't grown deep enough to resist the wind."

"That's very insightful," I said.

"The main point is that when you get your testimony of the Church, you'll join. I have faith in that."

"You know, I'm surprised you haven't become Catholic. I thought the hissing heater would have done you in by now," I told him.

"Hey, it'll take more than a hissing heater to bring down the Alaskan Mauler."

* * *

Fake Christmas trees had never appealed to me. Real ones were so much better. The fresh scent of pine, visiting local tree stands, and picking out the perfect

Elder P dressed as Santa.

tree helped make Christmas special.

But as I got older, fewer and fewer people enjoyed my annual tree-hunting expedition. They said I was too picky—the trees were either too tall or too short, too narrow or too fat. Sometimes they were too expensive, but I never did find a good one that was too cheap. Funny how some opposites are never a problem.

In more recent times, though, a subtle tide of change emerged. I had gone to Goodwill to see how far my money would stretch one December when I came upon a six-foot artificial Christmas tree. Here was the clincher. It was only six dollars—a dollar per foot. It didn't take a mathematician to figure out it was a bargain.

I've used that tree every year since, and it was the one I decorated in 2008. Not only did it please my mother, whose ability to discover bargains has amazed our family for years, but it also proved I was flexible. I had my opinions like anyone else, but when the right thing came along, I took it, even if it involved a little change. I was a reasonable, levelheaded person. The six-dollar tree proved it.

I had just finished decorating my bargain tree when the elders called. They wanted to stop in, and I said it was fine but requested they bring some of their Christmas pass-along cards. One or two would look nice on the tree, but Elder Bailey brought a dozen.

"I wasn't sure which one you wanted. Here are two different ones," he said, holding them out to show me.

One depicted Mary and Jesus in the manger with the words "joy to the world" written in cursive at the top. That was the one I pictured when I made my request.

In his other hand, Elder Bailey showed me a card of Jesus as an adult. He was standing in the doorway of his tomb with the stone rolled away. They were both beautiful depictions.

"I like them both. They'll look good on the tree," I said.

Elder Bailey tried to give me the cards, but I didn't accept.

"Why don't you and Elder P put them on?"

He handed half the cards to his companion, and the two went to work. Each elder took one side of the tree and searched for the best spots to place their pictures of Christ. I couldn't help but smile as I watched them. A boyish excitement took over those giants as they decorated the tree. They asked if they could move an ornament or two, and I said they could do whatever they liked.

If I had been thinking, I would have invited them over to decorate the tree from scratch, but missionaries rarely make time for such things. Too many people needed their attention, but with these two, it felt like they would have come to see me even if they weren't elders.

"We have a Christmas video we thought you might like," Elder P said. "It stars some famous old actor."

"Yeah, I think his name is Jimmy Stewart," Elder Bailey added.

"You guys are allowed to watch *It's a Wonderful Life?*"

"No, this is a video the Church made," Elder Bailey said.

I half expected them to say Jimmy Stewart was Mormon, but they didn't. We watched a movie made in 1980 called *Mr. Krueger's Christmas.* In it, Jimmy Stewart stars as a lonely old man who encounters a group of friendly carolers and dreams that he was present at the birth of Christ. Despite the main character's loneliness, he praises God and tells the baby Savior, in a conversation only the two of them hear, that Jesus is his best friend.

"The guy in the movie should have known those carolers were Mormon," I said as the credits rolled. "They were all rich. You could tell by the way they were dressed."

"Whatever," Elder Bailey scoffed.

"Dan, we're not rich. I had to work hard to save money for my mission," Elder P told me.

"I know. What kind of work did you do?"

"I did a lot of odd jobs. I worked a lot with my brother on stuff."

"What kind of odd jobs?" I asked.

"Like this one guy hired us to clear his land, so we had to move stones and throw rocks off his property."

"Wait a minute," Elder Bailey said. "Your job was to throw rocks?"

"Yeah."

"What was your title? Official Rock Thrower?"

Elder Bailey and I busted out in laughter. I'm pretty

sure he made all Elder P's future companion's aware of the rock-throwing past. And if you think about it, not many people can really claim that on their resume.

"What kind of work did you do, Elder Bailey?" I asked.

"I worked on the Alaskan pipeline for a while," he said.

"Wow, that sounds like a cool job."

"It sounds cooler than it was. But I mostly worked at Walmart."

Before they left, Elder P donned one of my Santa hats and a white beard that came from a wizard costume I wore at Halloween. We took pictures, and at first, I was far too short. A footstool cured the problem, and now I have several photos that make me look as tall as the Vikings.

I still have the pass-along cards the elders gave me that year. Every December, I put them on my tree and remember the Christmas season I spent with the missionaries. They're good memories—the kind that holidays are made of, and from what I understand, the elders still think about these things too. Rocks and all.

* * *

It was parents' night at catechism. My mother came, and we watched a movie about the life of Jesus. At one point, Sister Ruth paused the film to tell us that, unlike the actor playing him, Jesus probably didn't have blue eyes. Most people in the Middle East had brown eyes, so his eyes were probably brown.

It struck me as a strange commentary even at the time. We believed Jesus was born of the Virgin Mary, died on the cross, and was resurrected on the third day. But no way under heaven did He have blue eyes.

Which of these things was hardest to believe?

After the film, Sister Ruth gave each parent a red paper heart. It looked like a Valentine except it was cut into two even pieces. The parents had to take one half, and the kids the other. Sister Ruth instructed us to write something on our half of the heart that we forgave our parent for and vice versa.

We had learned earlier that Jesus forgave seventy times seven. Sister Ruth said it meant to always forgive, but I had quietly slipped my calculator out of my backpack when she wasn't looking. I was pretty sure this was one of those times when her interpretation wasn't right. I didn't want to forgive any more than what was required, after all. Seventy times seven sounded like plenty.

On my half of the heart, I wrote that I forgave my mother for interrupting my TV show. *Interrupt* was a big word back then, and I had to ask how to spell it. But it was the truth. Just when my cartoons were getting good, my mother had a bunch of silly questions that usually involved what I had eaten, what I wanted to eat, or when I wanted to eat it. If food was a Hollywood star, my mother was its paparazzi.

On her half of the heart, my mother wrote that she forgave me for being sassy. Let me state here and now that I have no idea what she was talking about. I'm innocent, I tell you. Innocent.

Sister Ruth came around again and handed out Band-Aids with the words "God's love" written on them. We were told to put our halves together and use the bandage to make the heart whole again.

It's one of the clearest memories I have of catechism, and I'm not sure why. For years, that heart was tacked to the wall in my bedroom. My mother had looked so serious when Sister Ruth talked about the Savior. She wanted God to be important to me just as He had always been to her. It's a lesson I've done my best to learn.

* * *

In 2009, the missionaries I knew were transferred, and my visits with the elders became less and less frequent. Eventually they faded out altogether.

My time with the missionaries may have ended, but we had a good run—one I'm grateful for to this day. And most of my elders still keep in touch from time to time.

Elder Luke went into the National Guard to help pay for college. He spent time stationed in Missouri and said he enjoyed the military life, except for a few of the knuckled-headed stunts some guys pulled off base. At one point, his unit held a grappling tournament, and Luke won first place. I told him Joseph Smith Jr. would be proud.

After his mission, Elder Childs returned to Maine with his parents for a short visit. His parents thanked me for being good to their son and praised the article I wrote about him back in 2007. As of this date, Childs is a student at Brigham Young University, and I suspect he's leaving a trail of broken hearts in his path. Watch out, ladies.

Meanwhile, Elder Kelsey's tailbone healed after he left Augusta. As a memorial to his accident, Elder Bailey hung the bent bike wheel in the living room of the Augusta missionary apartment. Last I knew, it was still there. A true symbol of caution if there ever was one.

As for me, I'm still searching. I'm still praying. In fact, my journey reminds me of something David Bednar, a leader in the LDS Church, once said.

At the October 2009 LDS general conference, he compared small acts of faith to the brush strokes in a

Elder Bailey holds the bike wheel that Elder Kelsey smashed in his accident. The elders tried to fix it, but this was the best they could do. Elder Bailey created the montage in the background during his tenure at the Augusta missionary apartment.

grand painting. You can't appreciate their significance up close. You have to step back to see how they all fit together. This story represents a few of the brush strokes I've made on the canvas of my life. It isn't complete because the painting isn't finished. I'm still working on it a little each day.

But my young elders taught me so much. I learned about a whole new faith and saw, for the first time, a religion and culture that blends so well into the American landscape that most people aren't aware it exists.

For many, the missionaries don't have faces. They're just name tags and neck ties, strangers to avoid at all costs. That's who they were for me too—a nebulous unit without individual thoughts, emotions, or motives.

My elders changed all that. They gave the Latter-day Saints a face, and it's my hope that this book will do for others what the elders did for me.

In my opinion, The Church of Jesus Christ of Latter-Day Saints is easy to dismiss on paper. But when you meet the people who believe in the Church, when they answer your questions honestly, and when you respect the way they live, you feel a power in their faith, that's hard to ignore.

I believe God wanted me to meet the missionaries. I'm still trying to understand why. Maybe it was to convert. Maybe it was to experience another side of faith. Or maybe, just maybe, it was to help others understand exactly who is at the door and what can happen if they open it.

EPILOGUE

I STARTED THIS BOOK BACK in 2007 with the intention of letting people know what it was like to be a missionary in America. Over time, an unexpected—sometimes unwanted—character crept into the story. That character was me.

I couldn't always understand what guys like Elder Luke or Dowling were thinking, but I knew how I felt. I realized that my voice—the voice of an investigator—often gets perfunctory treatment in the media. People are usually interested in outcomes, not journeys.

This memoir is interested in the journey.

The LDS audience is used to hearing conversion stories. It's what they expect, but we all know that life doesn't always meet our expectations. Some investigators don't join the Church. It's just reality. I saw it happen many times, and as those people left the pews, I quietly knew that was my fate too.

Call it arrogance. Call it naivety. But I didn't think anything the missionaries could say would make sense. I thought I could study them the way a scientist puts things in petri dish. Instead, I had to rethink a lot of what I believed, and it was not always a comfortable experience.

This tale is meant to be a human interest story. Battles over doctrine can be found everywhere, but a church is always more than its ideas or its ideals. It's also the people.

I don't think too many conversions hinge on how accurate the Book of Mormon may or may not be. People want a place to be accepted, a place to hear about God, a place where they feel God hears them. Simply put, most people aren't theologians. Neither am I. That's what we have in common.

I can't predict the future. Like most Christians, I want to be open to God and His will. But for me, some of the LDS Church's views were too different to embrace. At the same time, though, the elders had a positive impact on me. They opened the door to a different part of life, a new piece of the American pie. I met some great people and had some great opportunities because of the Church. In some ways, it was like a bank that I trusted. Although I had many good interactions with it, I just couldn't deposit my entire account there. It just wasn't my ending.

These days when I'm at Mass, I sometimes wonder what my elders are doing, what their lives are like, and how they've changed over the years. God loves them, just like He loves me. Understanding that is a step in the right direction. It's a step more people should take.

ABOUT THE AUTHOR

WHEN DAN HARRINGTON WAS EIGHT years old, he tried to interview a talking Rudolph the Red-Nosed Reindeer at Santa's Village in New Hampshire. With captivating questions such as "Exactly what Reindeer games do you play?" and "What's Santa favorite cookie?" he drove a teenage employee crazy enough to say that Rudolph was sleepy and had to go to bed.

Harrington became a professional freelance writer many years later in 2007. His work has appeared in publications such as *Village Soup*, *Kennebec Journal*, *Inside Pro Wrestling/The Wrestler*, *Portland Magazine*, and *LDS Church News*. He has written about everything from Mormon missionaries to extreme sports to law enforcement. *Who's at the Door? A Memoir of Me and the Missionaries* is his first book.